Activate Your Purpose:

A Guide to Spiritual

Goal Setting

Rosalind R. Sullivan

© 2018 Rosalind R. Sullivan

Published by Rosalind R. Sullivan
15224 Buchanan Court
Eden Prairie, MN 55344
www.rosalindrsullivan.com

Printed in the United States

All rights reserved. No part of this publication may be reproduced, stored in a retrieval system, or transmitted in any form by any means – for example, electronic, photocopy, or recording – without the prior written permission of the publisher. The only exception is brief quotations in printed reviews.

ISBN-13:
978-0692177099 (Rosalind R. Sullivan)

ISBN-10:
0692177094

Unless otherwise indicated, Scripture quotations are taken from the Holy Bible, New International Version.

Book cover and logo design by Xotic Design Firm, www.xoticdesignfirm.com

This book is dedicated to my three children

Shantell Nicole Buckhalton,

Amir Rashaad Trotter,

and

Cheo William Trotter

I wish I knew "then" what I know now. Raising the three of you has been my life's purpose for over 33 years! You are a blessing. You are all beautiful, talented, kind, humble; intelligent….simply phenomenal!

I love you dearly and I pray that this book will help each of you *Activate Your Purpose* on this earth.

TABLE OF CONTENTS

Acknowledgments	6
Introduction	8
The Purpose	13
Organization & Highlights	19
Chapter 1: Our Goals are Inspired by our Vision	25
Chapter 2: What are Spiritual Goals?	32
Chapter 3: The Importance of Spiritual Goal Setting	40
Chapter 4: Characteristics of Effective Spiritual Goal Setting	52
Chapter 5: Determining Your Spiritual Health	62
Chapter 6: Laying the Foundation	72
Chapter 7: Action Point #1: – Draw Close to God	82
Chapter 8: Action Point#2: – Walk in His Will	111
Chapter 9: Action Point#3: - Fish for People – Discipleship	129

Chapter 10:
Action Point#4: - Build Community					146

Chapter 11:
Putting it All Together					165

Works Cited							179

Author's Bio							180

~ Acknowledgements ~

This was a journey, taking several years before God would release me to move forward. There were people there from the very beginning and some along the way. I would like to thank everyone who contributed spiritually as well as financially to this project. I would like to thank and acknowledge my mother, Virginia Keyes, for believing that I can achieve anything. She has a strong foundation in God and raised us to always given Him honor. I would like to especially thank those who took the time to read my book including my daughter, Shantell Buckhalton, my sister, Anissa Keyes, my pastor, Pastor Darrell U. Gillespie and my dear friend Brittany Lane. These individuals read my book, provided in depth feedback, scripture references (and edits), prayer and encouragement. Anissa, Brittany and Shantell provided cover to cover, page by page edits, comments, and feedback. I am eternally grateful for your commitment and selflessness.

I want to thank the rest of my family, friends and church family (Proverbs Christian Fellowship Church); your prayers kept me going and will continue to keep me moving forward, never backward. I would also like to thank the members of *HER Story Ministries* Facebook Group, the ladies of *Latte* and the members, founder and admins of *Strictly for My Queens* Facebook Group for pushing me (allowing me to be derelict in my posting duties), encouraging me and believing in me from start to finish. I also must thank Dr. Mary Jo Winston and Bridges for Hope Leadership Academy for helping me to realize that I was indeed *pregnant with purpose*! Last, but certainly not least, I would like to thank Pastor Doris Allison for praying me through, encouraging me and standing in the gap for me during an extremely difficult time. When the enemy is on the attack, you <u>must</u> have spiritual warriors in your life that have your back no matter the fight. I would not have had the spiritual nor emotional strength to complete this assignment without you. Thank you!

~ Introduction ~

Although every experience is different, I would venture to say that when we are first born again we have an instant feeling of relief, elation and comfort. We are so in love with God and the "idea" of salvation that we are almost "giddy". However, it is very likely that at that moment many of us do not fully understand what it means to be saved or to be born again in Christ. We don't quite understand concepts like redemption, repentance, discipleship, the Kingdom of God and spiritual growth; we don't understand Purpose and its importance in our walk. We do however have a sense of God's omnipotence and his power to change our situation from bad to good. Sometimes this change is all we are looking for, this is what I call "surface salvation". We do not always know "how" to be a Christian. Contrary to what many new Christians believe, we actually have to "do" something; it does not stop with the washing away of our sins, that is just the beginning. Let me clarify my statement so as to not confuse or alienate anyone. The only thing that we <u>must</u> do in order to be born again is to believe in our heart and confess with our mouth that Jesus is Lord, repent from our sins and be forgiven. Baptism by water is an outward proclamation of that belief. This is what it means to be born again. Although there is nothing additional that we can do to gain access to the Kingdom of God, the Word of God does require more from us in order to stay in right standing with God. It is not by faith alone. *"God is not unjust; he will not forget your work and the love you have shown him as you have helped his people and continue to help him".* (Heb. 6:10). *"As long as it is day, we must do the work of him who sent me."* (John 9:4). It is clear that God has expectations about *how* we live our lives. In order for us to meet these expectations we must be proactive in *changing* our lives in a manner that is pleasing to God.

    Changing our life means becoming more like Christ. This can be a difficult concept for new Christians to grasp. Even "seasoned saints" may find themselves at a crossroads in their lives where they wake up one morning questioning their walk and wondering if there is more that God would have them to do. Being born again for a number of years does not mean that you are any more spiritually connected to God than a babe in Christ. In fact, sometimes discontentment, as seasoned saints may experience, stem from being disconnected from God and having failed to grow in their walk with Him. This is common when we lack of purpose. Although we will discuss the definition of spiritual goals later, in general, Spiritual Goal Setting is a process by which new saints can proactively begin their journey with Christ and where seasoned saints can redirect their journey. Spiritual Goal Setting is the process of discovering your purpose, getting direction from God and ultimately walking boldly in His will. This process allows you to be as proactive in your walk with God as you are in your business, job, sports, hobbies and financial endeavors. Doesn't God deserve the same focus and planning that goes into these other aspects of our lives?

As we seek to do God's will we may at times find ourselves questioning "how" we are to do God's will. God has a purpose for each and every one of us. His purpose for our lives will be revealed to us and the Holy Spirit will guide us. On our walk we must be proactive. We must live our lives ***on purpose; we must Activate Our Purpose***. God was very purposeful when He sent His Son to die on the cross for our transgressions. We must not look for direction from man to determine what we should do, how fast we should move or how we move at all as Christians. As God reveals his plan to us, we need to be mindful at all times that God wants us to seek Him. In seeking Him we must continue to do the things that He would have us to do. We set goals for our personal lives each day. In order to achieve Gods purpose for our lives, we must set spiritual goals that aid our growth and maturity in our walk. This book addresses the importance of spiritual goal setting, how to set and maintain these goals and ultimately how to grow in our relationship with Christ and achieve our purpose.

Many of us set New Year's resolutions each year. Unfortunately, many of us also break these resolutions before the month of January is even over. Resolutions are not necessarily a bad concept. However, many times they are unreasonable, unplanned and unachievable from the outset. Some of us would be more likely to succeed if the so called "resolutions" were actually well crafted goals based on a specific purpose with clearly delineated action steps. I would venture to guess that most of the resolutions revolve around material possessions, health, education, and money. These resolutions often tend to focus more on things of this world instead of our eternal life. Many of these resolutions also seek to accomplish goals that are temporary in nature and have little or nothing to do with the building up of the Kingdom of God. They tend to focus on the natural as opposed to the spiritual. I am not saying that we should not set natural goals, in fact; the better we are at setting natural goals the better we will be at setting spiritual goals. "So will it be with the resurrection of the dead. The body that is sown is perishable, it is raised imperishable; it is sown a natural body, it is raised a spiritual body. If there is a natural body, there is also a spiritual body." (1 Corinthians 15:42-44) It is my belief that in order for us to be successful witnesses and followers of Christ, we must set *spiritual goals* for our lives. Setting spiritual goals is a very intentional process that requires work on your part. The benefit will be enormous in our lives. It will bring about a transformational change in our relationship with Christ and others. Let's begin this journey together, let us Active Our Purpose!

~The Purpose~

"For I know the plans I have for you," declares the LORD, "plans to prosper you and not to harm you, plans to give you hope and a future." (Jer. 29:11)

The driving force behind this book was my own discontentment with myself as a Christian since the time that I rededicated my life to Christ. I felt like I made the commitment with my heart and was very serious about changing the person that I was. I began to do things that Christians "do". I started going back to church, attending Bible study, discipleship classes and other church events. I even became active in the women's ministry and eventually was assigned a leadership role over that ministry. I began to communicate with other Christians and even tried to make some friendship connections. I still felt that something was missing. I began to benefit from God's grace and mercy and I accepted his *various* gifts graciously. However, I was not giving God my full commitment and attention. I lacked a clear purpose and direction in my walk. I had no clue what my purpose was in His master plan.

As I became more involved in church I learned more about the word of God, I memorized the songs we sang every week and I even stopped doing some of the things that I "used to" do that I knew God was not pleased with. I certainly *felt* like I was on the right track, and I *believed* that I was. The problem is that we cannot just stay on the track just to be on the track. We have to know where the train is going, how fast it is moving, and be prepared for the layovers and stops along the way as well as the people who get on and off the train. If we don't, we are just along for the ride and we begin to even stop looking out the window because we are conditioned to just *ride*.

I began to pray for God to tell me what he wanted from me. He began to reveal some things that I was just not ready for. I did not know how to begin or if I wanted to begin. My life was consumed with my children and my business and church. I was simply too busy! As a small business owner my life was very busy. As a single parent of two young children at home (and one adult child with twin boys), life *was* chaotic. However, this busy and chaotic nature became a crutch and an excuse for ignoring the "unction" to do more for the body of Christ; to do more to uplift His Kingdom to grow deeper in my faith and closer to God. I knew all about goal setting as a business owner. I knew all about planning and meeting deadlines for my clients and making it all happen for the benefit of both my clients and my business. However, I did not seem to have the time or energy to commit the same amount of dedication to my walk with Christ that I did to my business. I believed that as long as I was doing a "good" thing that God would grant me favor, and he did, but He also burdened by heart with His desire for more from me.

    I knew that I had to be proactive in my walk. I knew that I had a call on my life for ministry but I floated around asking very surface questions as to *how* this was supposed to transpire. When it did not just "happen" through osmosis I figured it was just not meant to be or that God was not yet ready for me. As I continued to study and work in my church's women's ministry I began to set small goals for the women's ministry and my own personal growth. I began to see small changes in myself and my prayer life. The more I began to please Him the more I wanted to please him. God was pressing me forward to do more, to do his will the way he expected me to do it not the way I decided to do it. I began to have a true desire to please God. The more I prayed for direction, the more he gave it to me. The more I disobeyed that direction, the harder my walk became.

    I discovered that in order for me to truly live a life pleasing to God I needed to be proactive. I knew that I needed to give God the same attention, or more, than I gave my law practice. I gave clients my extra time. I did pro bono work, although sometimes unintentionally, as if I did not have a care in the world. I found time for those who needed my skills and advocacy. I even spent an insane amount of time in what I thought was "ministry" work. In order to truly walk in His will I had to make a conscious decision to take ACTION. My passion for Christ and my desire to be obedient to God, encouraged me to constantly seek Him in each and every thing I did. When I realized that ministry was serious business I began the goal setting process. I must admit, it was not easy. I found myself constantly reprioritizing God to fit into my life instead of reprioritizing my life to better serve His will. What I found, and thus the purpose for writing this book, was that I was much more effective when I acted purposefully, when I am proactive and when I took charge of my personal and business life through asking God to order my steps. When I did this, the doors began to open and life became so much clearer. When I opened myself up to this process, I was allowing God greater access to me and allowing the Holy Spirit to truly have free reign. Yes, the Holy Spirit can still have free reign when you are actively writing, setting and achieving clear goals. It's the "process" that you go through that allows you to get closer to God. It's the "process" that allows you to hear from God. It's the "process" that allows the Holy Spirit to have free reign. Goal setting does not contradict the Holy Spirit; it complements the Holy Spirit by allowing your ears, mind, and heart to be open and receptive when the Holy Spirit is speaking to you. I found that when I stumbled through the process and gave it even the least amount of energy, I benefited from it. I know that God speaks to me more frequently that I actually "hear" him. When I "hear" him I know that I am on the right track. When I have effectively prepared myself to actually do his will, then I know He is pleased.

I wrote most of this book over five years ago. I cannot believe how much time has passed. I asked God, why the delay? Why can't I seem to finalize this book? I prayed, edited, prayed and edited. I decided to locate a publisher, set the meeting, and signed the contract, this was in 2015. I went on a weekend stay-cation and finished the book. Yet, in 2017, I was in the same place. God said "you are not living the words you wrote!" I knew it; I had lost touch with the very basic concepts of the book, and everything around me, family, business and personal relationships were a clear indication of that. I began to re-write my goals, this time creating solid life goals. I read *Leading from the Inside Out: The Art of Self-Leadership* (Rima, 2000) with the ministerial team at church and began to draft my over-all life goals, which is an entirely different process. This gave me clarity on the purpose of the book for my own spiritual growth. I realized that I needed to revisit my own spiritual goals to accomplish my life goals. Even after this time of clarity, thing happened in my life that I did not expect. This time it was a battle against flesh and true purpose. I could clearly see the contradictions between the life I was living – the desires of the flesh – and the life of purpose. In spite of the setbacks, I was ready to begin again, to finally finish the product; to tell others how to *Activate Their Purpose*! The goal of this book is to "spark" to "activate" you to find your purpose in life. Following this goal setting process will indeed ignite that fire in you! I pray that you will "allow" this process to help draw you closer to God, enhance your walk and allow you to Activate Your Purpose. Peace and Blessings on your journey, Rosalind.

~ *Organization & Highlights* ~

The foundational focus of this book is on the areas of our lives goal setting is crucial, they are the cornerstones of spiritual goal setting. These will be discussed in detail later but I want to introduce you to them now. I call these four areas *Action Points*. Action Points is actually a business term used to describe a specific proposed action to be taken typically from a discussion or meeting. The term is used to define the key points or take-aways from a meeting in order to ensure that everyone present has a clear understanding of the tasks and the direction. The action points for spiritual goal setting are:

- ➢ #1: Drawing Closer to God
- ➢ #2: Walking in His Will
- ➢ #3: Fishing for People/Discipleship
- ➢ #4: Building Community

❖ *Key Scripture*

There are key verses at the beginning of each chapter that sum up the contents of the chapter. There will also be additional reference verses throughout each chapter. The Key Verse is one that you should read and become familiar with. It's also a great place to start your Bible study. When reading the verse in your Bible, be sure to read the verses and even the chapters before and after the Key Verse so that you have a full understanding of what was happening in the scripture at the time and the true meaning behind the verse, context is very important.

❖   *Reflection Questions*

Reflection questions are important, don't skip them. Answering them will help prepare you to set goals at the end of the book. These questions are meant to get you thinking and praying so that you can honestly and effectively set goals that are relevant to your life and God's revealed will. They will get you to think about your life, your purpose and your goals as you work through the Purpose Theme in the book.

❖   *Purpose Prayer*

There is a "Purpose Prayer" at the end of each section. Prayer is very personal so it may be difficult to get into the idea of a "scripted" prayer. However, God knows your heart. The purpose of these prayers are to help you know what to pray for and, for some of you, how to pray with purpose and clarity. Feel free to use the prayer or pray with your own words…the important thing is that you pray.

❖ Toolkit

There are certain tools that you will need to get the most out of this goal setting process. These tools are:

Time

If you read books for fun and information then you already very likely have a quiet place or a time of day that you read. I would suggest that you set aside time every day to read this book and to answer the reflection questions. I recommend writing your answers in a journal or notebook dedicated to Spiritual Goal Setting. Although the process of Spiritual Goal Setting is ongoing, you want to read the entire book over a short period of time and then take your time going over the goals, tweaking, editing and building on them as needed along your journey.

Bible

Your Bible is your weapon and should be carried with you at all times because you never know when you will need your weapon. "All scripture is God breathed and is useful for teaching, rebuking, correcting and training in righteousness, so that the servant of God may be thoroughly equipped for every good work." (2 Tim. 3:16). In the case of Spiritual Goal Setting, the word of God is your guide book to setting goals and you cannot set goals without having God's word. You will want to read the scriptures cited in this book for yourself. It is always important to know that what you read in any book lines up with the Word of God. You will need your Bible as you set your Spiritual Goals and to achieve the purpose that God has for your life. If you don't have one, get one today! I suggest a good study Bible, especially for those who may be new to reading the Bible.

Journal

Everyone is not the journaling type. I understand that. If you don't journal, think of it as note taking. Whether you call it note taking or journaling, writing down the answers to the reflection questions will allow you to really think about the concepts or issues presented in the book. It allows you to go back over and read what you wrote two weeks, two months or two years from now which can reveal true change or lack thereof. When you set your goals, writing them is essential to being able to carry out the goals. You will have a limited amount of space in this book to write the answers to reflection questions as well as your goals. However, I encourage you to use a second source, a notebook, journal, or whatever source of separate paper you have to record some of the information that you discover about yourself while reading this book. When you write the goals out you are much more likely to achieve them.

Accountability Partner(s)

Having someone else to help you in your process is not necessarily a requirement for Spiritual Goal Setting. However, it certainly makes a huge difference when it comes to actually working on and achieving your goals. An accountability partner should be someone you trust and someone that you have a good relationship with. Most of all, it should be someone who is spiritually mature. If you are a new Christian and have not developed a relationship with anyone in the church, seek out someone who is mature in Christ and that can and is willing and able to hold you accountable and willing to get to know you and become an empowering person in your life. This person needs to clearly understand the goals you are trying to reach and the steps you are taking to achieve the goals. Your accountability partner may even be able to help you find resources to help you achieve your goals. This person should be able and willing to pray for you, support you and be trusted with your process. It would be a plus to have this person go through the process as well. However, you may not necessarily be their accountability partner depending on where you are in your walk and whether you can provide the same support that person needs. The role of the accountability partner is important, so pray over whom that person should be and then have a conversation with them about what you are doing and whether they can support you and what you expect from them during this process. A note of caution, your accountability partner will not be setting goals for you. Be careful not to rely on anyone for specific direction, God is the one who will give direction.

~ Chapter 1 ~

Our Goals are Inspired by Our Vision

Key Verse

"Where there is no vision, the people perish: but he that keepeth the law, happy is he." (Prov. 29:18) (KJV)

We set goals to achieve some end. That end is basically our vision for our life. We must have a vision for our life. Without a vision, we go through life aimlessly; everyday is methodical without guidance or a plan. Many people have plans for their lives. We dream, we wish, we hope, we want…we develop some vague plan of where we want to be in life and at different times in our life. Sometimes we make broad statements like *"I want to be rich and famous"*, *"I want world peace"*, *I want to live a life pleasing to God"*, *"I want to be like Jesus"*. Whatever your vision is, you usually set goals, either formally or informally, to achieve that vision. The goals you set should be inspired by that vision.

Vision can be defined as:

Noun

1. The act or power of sensing with the eyes; sight.

2. *The act or power of anticipating that which will or may come to be*: *prophetic vision; the vision of an entrepreneur.*
3. An experience in which a personage, thing, or event appears vividly or credibly to the mind, although not actually present, often under the influence of a divine or other agency: *a heavenly messenger appearing in a vision.*
4. Something seen or otherwise perceived during such an experience: *The vision revealed its message.*
5. A vivid, imaginative conception or anticipation: *visions of wealth and glory.* (https://www.merriam-webster.dictionary/vision)

The relevant definition here is the bolded one above, "**the act or power of anticipating that which will or may come to be**". Vision is the "act" of anticipating what we want; even our vision is an action statement. When we visualize something we see it coming to fruition, we see it being real. This vision is our desire for our lives whether it is short term or long term. Some of us may not have a vision for our lives. Having a vision is crucial as our vision is what guides our actions, as well as our reactions, as we navigate life. The act or power of anticipation means not only that we dream but we act in accordance with our dreams. For example, in the natural a person's vision may be to become the greatest athlete of all times. A person with this vision would treat his or her body well by eating nutritious foods, working out daily, and avoiding drugs or other chemicals that might hinder her vision. Our vision for our natural lives can be no greater than God's will for our spiritual and natural lives. We must seek God first and be willing to submit to him even if it's contrary to what we "think" our vision is. Once you know what His will is for your life you can begin to develop a real vision for your life. We basically desire to please God in all that we do. We can use that as our very broad, overall <u>vision</u> for the Christian life. With that vision in mind, you know that you must "do" something; you must act a certain way in order to please God. You cannot achieve this vision by being idle.

A great example of vision can be seen through Paul's experience. In Philippians Paul talks about His ultimate vision. "Not that I have already obtained all this, or have already been made perfect, but I press on to take hold of that for which Christ Jesus took hold of me. Brothers, I do not consider myself yet to have taken hold of it. But one thing I do: Forgetting what is behind and straining toward what is ahead, I press on toward the goal to win the prize for which God has called me heavenward in Christ Jesus." (Phil. 3:12-14) Paul's goal was to know Christ, to be like Christ and to be all Christ would have Him to be. This was Paul's vision and his actions, words, and behaviors all lead him closer to that vision.

We can all take on Paul's global vision as our own vision for the purpose of setting goals and living our lives on purpose. Therefore, the vision for which we will set goals is *to know Christ, to be Christ-like and to be all Christ would have me to be.* This is our working vision for purpose of this book and these exercises.

Our *ultimate* vision has been predetermined by God. He has a predetermined plan for our lives. Because we will be using the global vision of living a life pleasing to Christ, we will not prepare a personal vision statement as part of this reading. However, I encourage you, as you work through this book, to begin drafting a personal vision statement for your life. In this text, we will explore some basic concepts regarding purpose, and. Therefore; we will use Paul's vision as our over-all vision. At some point you will have to create over-all life goals but this is outside of the scope of this book. No matter what your vision is or what God's plan is for your life, the principles in this book will support, enhance and even ignite your ultimate vision and destiny. We must act a certain way in order to please God. We cannot achieve anything without God. We cannot achieve our goals by being idle! God expects us to move in our gifts, to constantly seek direction and act upon that direction and to grow daily in Him.

God will reveal his ultimate vision for our lives if we seek Him. "But if from there you seek the Lord your God, you will find him if you look for him with all your heart and with all your soul." (Deut. 4:29) Use this opportunity to seek God's vision for your life for His vision will stand firm. "For he spoke, and it came to be; he commanded, and it stood firm. The Lord foils the plans of the nations; he thwarts the purposes of the peoples. But the plans of the Lord stand firm forever, the purposes of his heart through all generations." (Psa. 33:9-11).

Does Goal Setting Contradict Walking in God's Will?

The answer is, absolutely not. Goals help us to achieve our vision. There may be some critics who say that planning, through spiritual goal setting, somehow hinders the Holy Spirit from moving in your life. However, the Word of God itself dispels that assertion. Luke 14:28 contains a teaching by Jesus and reads "Suppose one of you wants to build a tower. Will he not first sit down and estimate the cost to see if he has enough money to complete it? For if he lays the foundation and is not able to finish it, everyone who sees it will ridicule him, saying, "This fellow began to build and was not able to finish." One commentary on this story is that as Christians, we must count the cost of being a Christian and a disciple for Christ. However, another consideration is that we must understand that before we begin this journey we have to reflect not just on the cost but our own abilities, weaknesses, strengths and purpose before attempting to build our Christian life. If we don't first make this assessment and discover our weaknesses and begin to strengthen ourselves allowing us to grow, our own foundation will be weak: this decreases our ability to heed the Holy Spirit in the first place. This is as starting point for everything we do in our life. The purpose of this book is to get you to Activate Your Purpose – make active the will of God in your life. This begins with your active participation in seeking Him. He will bless you, guide you, lead you and reveal thing to you throughout this process.

When I first started writing this book I prayed a great deal about the topic, the process and the purpose. My vision for the book was to provide a guide for others to be purposeful in their spiritual development process. I knew that this was a vision supported by God because he has equipped me with the skills and experiences necessary to make it happen. However, as I started to write I noticed that I got stuck. Months would pass before I could write again. I was confused as to why God had stopped the process. I realized that I had veered away from my own spiritual goals and it was not until I began to notice this misalignment that I truly understood the problem. God expects order. The Holy Spirit convicted me as I was out of order. It was my responsibility to make a plan of action to get back on track with the vision. Getting back on track required purposeful planning on how I was going to address the goals that I had failed to reach, how I was going to realign myself with God's will and eventually, how was going to accomplish the finished product that you are now reading.

Spiritual Goal Setting allows us to Activate Our Purpose and the result is Living our Lives on Purpose for Christ! God honors order and diligence.

~ Chapter 2 ~
What Are Spiritual Goals?

Key Verse

"So then, just as you received Christ Jesus as Lord, continue to live in him, rooted and built up in him, strengthened in the faith as you were taught, and overflowing with thankfulness." (Col. 2:6-7)

Spiritual Goals are simply goals we set regarding our spiritual life, more specifically, they are the goals we set in order to strengthen our walk with Christ and live a life pleasing to God. Spiritual Goals Active You Purpose. It is important to examine the two words carefully before moving forward into a full discussion of spiritual goals.

GOAL(S)

Goals, in general, have both specific and broad reaching implications for our lives. We set goals every day of our lives. We set goals regarding our educational aspirations, we set goals for weight loss and health, we set goals for saving (or spending) money etc. Goals have a very important place in our lives. As Christians, goals are just as important to set. The word *goal* is defined as:

> *Goal(s)* – are a projected state of affairs that a person or a system plans or intends to achieve – a personal or organizational *desired end point* in some sort of assumed development. *A desire or an intention becomes a goal if and only if one activates an action for achieving it.*

This definition distinguishes between "desires" and "goals". We desire many things both spiritually and naturally. But desires are not goals; they are just emotional ideas that do not suggest any action or plan for their achievement. Desires only become goals when we ACT upon them. Acting requires a plan. For example; as a minister, I have a desire to be able to pray for the sick and have compassion for them as I minister to both their body and their soul. I desire a deep connection with those that I am praying for. This is something good to desire. However, if I want to actually be able to accomplish this I must begin to pray for the spirit of discernment. I must read my Bible so that I have the power of the Word of God to use when and how necessary. I must also begin to develop relationships with people and listen to their stories so that I can understand where they have been in order to develop true compassion for what they are going through. God grants certain gifts. He wants you to be fully prepared to use them and being fully prepared does not happen by chance. I believe that it requires a plan of action which begins with setting clear goals

SPIRIT(UAL)

In this book we will focus on spiritual goals as opposed to natural goals. In order to understand the difference, we will first discuss spiritual as it relates to this book.

> **Spirit -** (Heb. ruah; Gr. pneuma), *properly wind or breath*. In 2 Thess. 2:8 it means "breath," and in Eccl. 8:8 *the vital principle in man*. It also denotes the *rational, immortal soul by which man is distinguished* (Acts 7:59; 1 Cor. 5:5; 6:20; 7:34), and *the soul in its separate state* (Heb. 12:23), and hence also an apparition (Job 4:15; Luke 24:37, 39), an angel (Heb. 1:14), and a demon (Luke 4:36; 10:20). *This word is used also metaphorically as denoting a tendency* (Zech. 12:10; Luke 13:11).
>
> In Rom. 1:4, 1 Tim. 3:16, 2 Cor. 3:17, 1 Pet. 3:18, it designates *the divine nature*. (Eatons Bible Dictionary)

In reviewing the biblical definition of spirit above, I have bolded the pieces of the definition that stand out. Our spirit is our vital principle, our divine nature. *"...It is sown a natural body, it is raised a spiritual body. If there is a natural body, there is also a spiritual body."* (1 Cor. 15:44). Our spiritual self is what connects us to God. It is our divine nature that God works with. It is the part of us distinguishable from our flesh and the desires of our flesh. Our spirit is what makes us different from all other creatures on the Earth. Man's spirit, when indwelt with God's spirit, becomes a focal point of worship. In the word spiritual the suffix 'ual' denotes "relating to". It turns the word spirit into an adjective. An adjective describes the word following it in a sentence. If we take a look at the English language definition we get the following:

> **Spir·i·tu·al** *adj.* **1.** Of, relating to, consisting of, or *having the nature of spirit; not tangible or material.* See Synonyms at immaterial. **2.** Of, *concerned with, or affecting the soul.* **3.** Of, from, or *relating to God*; deific. **4.** Of or belonging to a church or religion; sacred. **5.** Relating to or having the nature of spirits or a spirit; supernatural. (The American Heritage Dictionary of the English Language, 2009)

The two definition sets have similarities as they separate the man's spirit from his material or natural self. For the purposes of this book, we will combine the Bible dictionary definition with the English dictionary definition and other sources to form a working definition of the word spiritual:

> *Spiritual* - the vital principle in man…relating to, consisting of, or concerning the soul, not tangible or material…supernatural.

Therefore, we conclude that spiritual has to do with our life as it relates to God not as it relates to ourselves. Being "spiritual" in a sense is the development of an individual's inner life and their relationship with God through practices that strengthen the spirit. Spirituality, as the word relates to Christians, begins with our ultimate gift from God, which is Jesus Christ. Jesus Christ came to free us from certain worldly rules, laws, rituals and traditions set forth in the Old Testament. This gave us freedom and the ability to "walk in the spirit". This ultimately allowed us to establish and maintain our Christian lifestyle through a one-on-one relationship with God.

God intended for us to have a new spirit, one that is stayed on Him and His will for our lives. In order for it to be new, we have to work at it, we have to develop our spiritual selves and that requires us to be proactive; it requires action.

Let's examine the difference between spiritual and worldly or the term natural. When we sit down with our family and make a budget for our household we consider things like income, expenses, upcoming vacations and travel, educational expenses, possible job loss anticipation etc. In comparison, when we think about our spiritual self we think about how effective we are in praying for the income and that the dollars we bring into our home be stretched beyond the human realm of possibility. Spiritual is asking God to increase that dollar. Spiritual is tithing and asking God to use this money in a mighty way without expecting a personal benefit from our sacrifice. Spiritual is asking God whether you should accept a certain job or whether you should seek out a certain educational opportunity. One could argue that natural and spiritual goals are one in the same, in fact inseparable. I agree. When we are setting financial, marital and educational goals we must consult God. We must make sure our plans, activities, desires and goals line up with God's will for our lives. I wholeheartedly promote this. This book does not negate that principle. The goal is to get us to focus much less on the natural and use this book as a

> "Rid yourselves of all the offenses you have committed, and get a new heart and a new spirit..." (Eze. 18:31)

tool to hone in on the spiritual, taking time off from the day to day issues of the world and focus on God and how we can be true, living, sacrifices for Him. In the end, it will enhance our ability to effectively set goals in every area of our lives.

Now that we have discussed the words separately, let's analyze them together. If we put the two definitions of "spiritual" and "goal together we can develop a working definition of a *"spiritual goal"*.

> ***Spiritual Goal*** – An internally desired endpoint, separate from material or tangible desires that seek to enhance the natural tendency to grow closer to God. These desired endpoints are achieved through active participation in, and association with, activities, people, places and events that build up the Kingdom of God.

When we are at the point in our lives where we are considering setting spiritual goals for ourselves, we are *seriously* seeking God. We must seek God's will for our lives before we begin the goal setting process. Setting goals is so important that we don't want to set goals according to what **we** want from our Christian walk; we must seek **God's will** for our lives and actively find a way to strengthen our ability to meet that end. It is critical that we understand God's will and that He in fact has a plan for our lives. God has a will for each and every one of us. He knew us before we were born. He has predestined us for greatness. We will discuss this in more detail in the section on *Walking in His Will.*

If you have not already done so, now is the time to get your journal. Before moving forward, write this question in your journal or use the space provided. *Am I living a life pleasing to God?* No matter what your answer is, write it down. After you write your answer, explain why you answered the way you did. Write down at least three "reasons" for your answer. No matter what answer you gave or the reasons for your answer, you can benefit from spiritual goal setting. Use this question, and answer, as a springboard for the spiritual goal setting process. Reflect back on your written response to this question before you set your goals at the end of the book.

Reflection Question #1:
Am I living a life pleasing to God?

_____
_____
_____
_____

~ Chapter 3 ~
The Importance of Spiritual Goal Setting

Key Verse
"Every prudent man acts out of knowledge; but a fool exposes his folly."
(Prov. 13:16)

Why set specific goals when we can just promise ourselves, and God, that we will do better? Why set spiritual goals if God truly already knows our heart and our destiny? What does it have to do with purpose? Spiritual Goal Setting is not for God, it is for us to increase the likelihood that we will meet His expectations for our lives. Spiritual goals are more important than any other goals we set for our lives. If we really think about it, what could be more important than setting a goal for God based on His will for our life? What can be more important than getting to know God and doing His will? Our spiritual lives set the foundation for our natural lives. When our natural lives are guided by the spirit of Christ, our natural lives will be in tune with God's will. The definition of purpose is pretty basic. Purpose is simply the reason for which something is done or created or for which something exists. In order for us to understand the purpose for which we exist, we must be connected to the one who ceated us. The process described in this book focuses on that connection. To understand your purpose you must know that creator. Let's discuss the practical importance of Spiritual Goal Setting.

- **Spiritual Growth**

    Spiritual growth means maturity in Christ and His word, maturity in dealing with and conquering the wiles of the enemy, growth in the knowledge of His word and understanding of God's character. This almost encompasses <u>all</u> the following reasons we need to set spiritual goals. When we set and reach spiritual goals the result is spiritual <u>growth</u>.

- **Getting Closer to God**

    Spiritual goal setting allows us to learn more about God and in that learning we get an understanding and with an understanding our faith is increased and when we are faithful we grow closer to Him and begin to trust Him even more. As we get closer to God, we develop a close personal relationship with God that surpasses all natural relationships. Close fellowship with God gives us power to minister and defeat the enemy's devices; it encourages our obedience to Him.

- **Concrete Plans**

    Just as we may develop plans for a job, plans to pay off bills and plans to send children off to college, it's just as crucial to develop a concrete plan for our spiritual lives. Setting goals allows you to develop concrete plans for your Christian "walk" as opposed to just saying "I'll do better" or "I will try harder". When we have a concrete plan as to how we are going to increase the quality of our spiritual lives, the more likely we are to have the success we desire and to please God. Failing to have concrete plans makes us much more vulnerable to falling out of fellowship with Christ.

- **<u>Adds Meaning to Your Life</u>**

Setting spiritual goals gives us a roadmap to live for Christ and it adds meaning to our lives. As we set goals we begin to work on the ***how*** and the ***when*** of spiritual growth. We will begin to study more and seek out other people as we develop action plans for our goals. Our lives will begin to finally take shape and form and we will begin to activate our true purpose; we will actually want to accomplish the goals that we set and look forward to achieving them. The Spiritual Goal Setting process gives hope and meaning to our lives. Some of us may really believe that our life has meaning and that we are on the right track because the world tells us so. However, nothing adds meaning to our life like living for God. If we take this process seriously and apply ourselves, we cannot help but find new meaning in our life; you cannot help but *activate our purpose*.

- **Faster Route to Manifesting your Desires**

  The natural outcome of goal setting is that we develop a plan for achieving the goals that we set. This is much more effective than just "wishing" or even praying. God has given us great ability and knowledge and He expects us to use these gifts for His benefit. Setting goals allows us to get where we need to be <u>faster</u> and more <u>effectively</u> in that if we follow this process, you know that we are walking in His will. We can often avoid some of the pitfalls that one may experience in life. Sometimes we find ourselves in a rut or look up and ask why we have not grown or why it's taking so long to learn God's word. If we set goals we are much more likely to see quicker progress in our spiritual growth. Now the disclaimer – we must remember that God's time is not like our time. I am not saying that this is a race, in fact, it is a marathon. What I *am* saying is that there should be definite "progress" more so than "speed". There are some of us who have been born again for many years and are still not living in the fullness of God's will for our lives. This is certainly not uncommon. Setting spiritual goals can help to avoid that kind of "lost" time and missed opportunity to serve God fully.

- **Live life on Purpose by Activating Your Purpose**

  Living our lives on purpose is key to every aspect of our time on this Earth. When we direct our own path instead of allowing the economy, family, friends and government to do so, we can live life more abundantly. As I mentioned in the introduction, when I was floating around trying to be the best Christian I could be, I was failing. I was disconnected because I did not have direction, I lacked purpose. I was allowing people to tell me, "Oh you did well this morning with the sermon" or "I enjoyed the women's conference" but I did not do enough to take control over what I was going to do at any moment. I did not have a plan and I did not set goals to achieve the things I knew that God wanted me to do. We cannot just *will* things to happen. God created us too intricately for us to not use what we have been given. We must activate our purpose in order to live according to God's will. Part of living life on purpose is also acknowledging our faults and short comings. When we write these things down we can set goals that take into consideration our short comings and seek to educate ourselves to overcome these shortcomings. Even the process of identifying faults can be empowering. Nobody wants to be a slave to sin but many of us live unknowing that we are slaves to sin because we are not living our life on purpose. We do things for the sake of doing them, even good things, but we don't pray for direction and don't pray for purpose. When we set spiritual goals we take control, under the guidance and direction of the Holy Spirit, of how we live our life, how we react to things, people, and situations and how we grow, mature and develop in Christ. We don't have to wait for direction from anyone but God when we Activate Our Purpose.

- **Measureable results**

    As we know the best laid plans can go astray. When you have actually set goals and developed action plans to achieve the goals, it's much easier to determine where you went off track as well as checking to see if our actions are still in line with our goals. If we don't have a way to "check" ourselves; we may not even know that we are off track until we have gone so far off course that it takes even more work to get back where we should be. It is absolutely rewarding and encouraging to know that we have achieved our goal. It is even more important to know where and when we need a little help or change of direction. In order to measure success, we must have a tool to do so. Without having set goals, we cannot measure our success. First and foremost, God is the one true measuring stick. However, again we are talking about developing spiritual goals through prayer that support God's will for our life, we don't set spiritual goals in isolation or without God. If the goal is succinct and specific it is easier to measure the results. From a spiritual stand point our "fruit" is a good measure of whether we are achieving or have achieved our spiritual goals. In the context of this book "fruit" means the product of our faith and work in the name of Jesus. We do however need to understand the difference between good fruit and bad fruit. Just because we achieved some significant things in life does not necessarily mean that we have "achieved" our goals. Further, it does not mean that we are walking in step with God's plan for our life. An example of why it is important that a goal be measureable is reflected in the following two statements (1) My Goal is to Read the Bible or (2) My Goal is to Study the Word of God by Reading at least 10 minutes per day. The first goal is great; we all need to read and study the word of God. However, the second goal is more specific in that this goal emphasizes "study" over just "reading" and sets a goal for how much time will be committed to studying the word each day. Therefore, when you are four months into the activity there are two ways to measure your results. First, whether you actually know more about the Word than you did when you started and second, whether you actually studied 10 minutes per day. One is a qualitative measurement and one is a quantitative measurement. Goal #2 is measureable. We cannot measure every goal quantitatively, but each goal should be drafted in a way that allows for success or accomplishment to be measured. The true measurement is whether God is pleased with you and what you have allowed Him to do through us. Whether God is pleased will be reflected in your good fruit, the Holy Spirit's presence in your process and whether God allows you to stay on the track that you are on.

- **<u>Increased likelihood of Success</u>**

    Setting clear spiritual goals absolutely and unequivocally increases the likelihood that we will achieve our desired goals. I am absolutely convinced that if you follow the concepts in this book, you will achieve what you desire, as long as what you "desire" is in line with God's will for our life. Just the fact that you have purchased this book and have the desire to live our life on purpose for God will positively impact your success. This process will activate our purpose.

When I was editing this book my sister asked me whether Spiritual Goal Setting makes living for Christ easier. I was intrigued by the question because when you think of setting goals you set them for many reasons which we have discussed above. However, "easier" is such a relative term. I think that living for Christ is a difficult concept for most of us to grasp. I also believe that we fail, we fall, we sin and we fail to grow and mature because we don't activate our Purpose. I also believe that when we do Activate our Purpose our path becomes clearer, we understand God's will for our life so we are more likely to act in accordance with his will; so in that respect I do think that living for Christ is *easier* when we set spiritual goals.

Reflection Question #2:

How do you think setting spiritual goals will impact your personal walk with Christ?

_____

_____

_____

Why We Fail to Set Spiritual Goals

If we know how important spiritual goal setting is, why don't most people set spiritual goals for their life? Why do people continue for years through their Christian "walk" and never map out a plan for their spiritual life and spiritual growth? Why do people spend each December making New Year's resolutions about money, love and education but fail to make specific goals for your own salvation? There are numerous reasons why we do what we do. However, here are a few very common reasons that most of you can relate to:

- <u>*Never really thought about it*</u> – It's understandable that many of us have just never thought about it before. We don't always look at our spiritual life as something that we need to <u>plan; it's</u> something that we just "do". However, there are really very few things in life that we "just do". In fact, most of us actively plan all or most areas of our lives in some capacity but we just don't think about the importance of planning our spiritual life or spiritual growth.

- <u>*Fear of failure or Inability to reach set expectations*</u> – Setting a goal is concrete and it's easy to see when we have failed or missed the mark. Sometimes we think that if we don't set a goal or if we don't aspire to anything that we cannot fail. We live in fear of failure so we just don't put ourselves in a position to fail. I must admit, setting goals makes you accountable. Once we write something down it becomes real and it's very difficult to ignore. The good part is that there is no failure in this process, <u>only success</u>. When we set our mind on improving our spiritual health there is no such thing as failure. We get "do over's" and "rewrites" in this process. The focus is always on God, His will and His way.

- *Self-indulgence* – Some of us are so caught up in the day to day that we don't focus on the eternal. We even forget that there is such a thing as an "eternal". When we look at our lives we plan for the week by purchasing food and paying the bills. We focus on saving money for the cruise that we have never been on. But what if you lose your job? What would happen to all of these worldly plans if your spouse or child dies? Our salvation is more important than any of those things and how we live our spiritual lives will help us get through all natural life issues including crisis, death and other unexpected circumstances. We get so caught up in the natural that we lose complete focus on our spiritual life.

- *Lack of goal setting knowledge* – Many of us do not set goals in the natural so it is very difficult to conceptualize setting spiritual goals. This makes the process much more difficult. However, this book is more of a workbook, allowing you to use the same information and process to set natural goals. It is very important to use goal setting in _every_ aspect of your life.

- *Lack of Maturity in our Faith* – Some of us desire to be better stewards but our newness in Christ does not always afford the opportunity to know what we should and should not do. Lack of maturity can also occur in those "seasoned saints". Just because you have been born again for a long period of time does not mean that you are "mature". Maturity comes through prayer, faith, practice, studying the word of God, being challenged, fellowship, discipleship and of course, spiritual goal setting. Don't let lack of maturity keep you from moving forward and *continuing* to grow in Christ. There is no such thing as reaching the *top* of spiritual maturity. Now is the time for you to 'grow' up and become a mature saint, no matter how long you have been born again. In fact, now is the *perfect time!*

Reflection Question #3: Why have you failed to set spiritual goals for your life? If you have set goals, what has hindered you the most from achieving your goals?

_____
_____
_____
_____
_____

~ Chapter 4 ~

Characteristics of Effective Spiritual Goals

Key Verse

"So we make it our goal to please him, whether we are at home in the body or away from it."

(2 Cor. 5:9)

Setting spiritual goals is somewhat of a science. There are certain characteristics of an effective goal that increase the chances of the goal actually being achieved. These characteristics are as follows:

Spiritual Goals must be:

Christ Centered

"And we know that in all things God works for the good of those who love him, who have been called according to his purpose" (Rom. 8:28) It is crucial that your goals be centered on what Christ has planned for your life. We must pray for direction before even beginning the goal setting process. Our goals should line up with God's plans for our life or they are destined to fail. Even if we don't know the plan, we can always set goals to get to know God better…we cannot go wrong with such a goal.

Reinforced by Prayer

Jesus' disciples asked *"Lord teach us to pray."* (Luke 11:1). We must pray for understanding. We must pray for each goal that we set so that you may hear from God. We must pray for His will to be done; we must pray as we write in order to get guidance in developing our spiritual goals and we must pray over the goals that they are fulfilled for the uplifting of the Kingdom and that God get the glory.

Realistic

Goals must always be realistic. Reading the Bible is a realistic goal; although very broad. Reading the Bible in one month is generally an unrealistic goal. I will stop sinning in 21 days is not realistic. Sometimes saying I will attend church every Sunday is not realistic, but for the person who is generally consistent but misses periodically it could be a very realistic goal to set. Whether a goal is realistic is relative to the person and God's will. Set goals that are realistic for you to achieve based on where we are in our lives. Also, what we sometimes think is unrealistic may be something that God will make happen in spite of our actual or perceived ability. Therefore, be careful not to set limits on God when we are setting goals, especially when He has given us specific direction in an area.

Achievable in a Specific Time Frame

Although living for Christ is a lifelong process, goals should have a specific time frame. Most goals will have a time frame. For example, you need to be specific as to how long it will take you to begin to attend church regularly or when you will begin attending a formal Bible study group. However, some goals will be achievable only over a longer undetermined period of time depending on the nature of the goal. For example, our overall vision is to live a life pleasing to God. This is a process that may take a life time. The goal to become more knowledgeable about God is a little more specific and will help us achieve our vision. However, this goal will take a period of time to "accomplish". As we mature in Christ, our goals, and the time frames for achieving them, will change. For example, if it is your goal to read the Bible consistently, set a goal outlining how much you will read and how long you will read and the purpose or focus of your reading. If it is your goal to finish a certain chapter or book set a time frame that is achievable without the added stress and pressure on your time. In general, our goals must have a time frame for completion or at least a range associated with the action step.

Specifically-Articulated

"The plans of the diligent lead to profit as surely as haste leads to poverty". (Prov. 21:5) Our goals must be specific. Our overall vision for our lives may be broad, for example, you may have a vision to minister to those that are the hardest to reach and have yet to hear the word of God. This is a very broad vision that can certainly be accomplished. However, the goals we set to reach that vision are crucial. For example, a possible goal in relation to the example above may be to develop a curriculum that can be studied by people who have no prior exposure to Christ. This is specifically articulated and as we take action to reach those individuals we will have the tools necessary to accomplish our mission and eventually achieve our vision. The more specific the goal, the easier it is to create action steps for the goal.

Evaluated Periodically

We should always evaluate our goals periodically. As we pray, plan and mature in Christ, God may reveal the plans He has for us and they may not be consistent with our goals, especially if we were either not prayerful when we set them or just were not sure if we were hearing from God at the time. The key step in evaluating is periodically asking God to confirm that we are on the right track. Look at our goals to see if we are having difficulty achieving them; are there roadblocks that keep getting in the way of us achieving our goals? If so, we may be moving in the "good" direction but not God's direction. The positive outcome is that we were *moving* and actively seeking God with every step. Being a willing vessel, flexible and ready to be used by God is a great place to be even if it involves a re-write. If you hear from God and he tells you that you are on the wrong track and you need to re-write your goals you should be praising God that He sees your willingness and is speaking to you loud and clear and giving you clear direction for your life. If you check your goals and actions and God says you are on the right track, keep moving forward. God may give you the green light through using the Holy Spirit to confirm His Will, giving you the strength, knowledge and the tools to do what you are doing and by increasing your output - your fruit.

Prioritized

We all have priorities in life. Some things are more important than others. This may seem like common sense. The only problem that we run into with prioritizing is when we are juggling multiple tasks and responsibilities in our lives. We are busy people. We may have to determine which goals are the most important as it's very unlikely that we can fully achieve multiple goals at the same time. There are also things that *should* be prioritized over other things even if we do not want to. For example, it may be very important for us to get an accountability partner, in fact it may be a priority given our current spiritual situation. Due to our own fear we put this last on our list to avoid having to actually be held accountable. Goals must be prioritized in order of importance, time and rationality for establishing the goal. How you prioritize depends on where you are in your spiritual walk. Goals that have to do with your own spiritual development may take priority over being your "brother's keeper". I say this because before you can understand the expectation and the commitment needed to truly be your "sister's keeper", you have to understand who God is and what He expects from you and why. Once you have set your goals, go back and rank them according to what is important to you as revealed by the Holy Spirit.

Validated by other Christians

"Plans fail for lack of counsel, but with many advisers they succeed." (Prov. 15:22), "For where two or three come together in my name, there am I with them." (Matt. 18:20) We need each other to survive! You must seek out other Christians and share your goals. As I indicated earlier, you at least have to have one accountability partner to help validate your goals and assist you with your process. Get counsel from your leaders, elders or pastors in the goals that you have set. You may find that they have also set goals; they may have resources and most importantly can pray for you in your process and hold you accountable for your goals when they see that you are having difficulty staying on track. One caution I have is to never allow people to invalidate what God has already given you. Always seek Him first and other Christians second. When seeking out other Christians, make sure they are mature and that they will in turn pray for discernment as they advise you in your process.

Consistent with Other Life Goals

Spiritual goals should actually be incorporated into your personal/natural goals. Although spiritual goals in general are the goals that we set that impact our spiritual nature, they must be consistent with our natural life goals. If you are ineffective in planning your day or week or planning for your financial future, you will find it very difficult to plan for your spiritual life. Use the same process to set natural goals that support the development of your physical, mental, social and financial health. If you are disorganized and are not financially sound, it will impact your ability to accomplish your spiritual goals.

> "The spiritual did not come first, but the natural and after that the spiritual." 1 Cor. 15:46

Must Include Submission to God

"Now listen, you who say, 'Today or tomorrow we will go to this or that city, spend a year there, carry on business and make money.' Why, you do not even know what will happen tomorrow. What is your life? You are a mist that appears for a little while and then vanishes. Instead you ought to say 'if it is the Lord's will, we will live and do this or that.' As it is you boast and brag. As such boasting is evil. Anyone, then, who knows the good he ought to do and doesn't do it, sins." (Jam. 4:13-16)

All of your spiritual and natural goals must involve complete submission to the will of God. No matter how positive and good our goals are, they must line up with the will of God. In order to know the will of God, we must submit to Him in *all* things. An effective spiritual goal requires submission to the will of God.

Recap

The Characteristics of Effective Spiritual Goal

- ✓ Christ Centered
- ✓ Reinforced by Prayer

- ✓ <u>Realistic</u>
- ✓ <u>Achievable in a Specific Time Frame</u>
- ✓ <u>Specifically Articulated</u>
- ✓ <u>Evaluated Periodically</u>
- ✓ <u>Priorities</u>
- ✓ <u>Validated by other Christians</u>
- ✓ <u>Consistent with Other Life Goals</u>
- ✓ <u>Must Include Submission to Christ</u>

Reflection Question #4:

Before we get started, let's practice on your personal goal setting ability. Draft three personal goals that you have for your life. Then draft three spiritual goals that you have for your life. I know that we have not discussed in detail how we are going to draft spiritual goals but I want you to practice started now and then you can edit as needed in later chapters.

Natural Goals:

(1) _____

(2) _____

(3) _____

Activate Your Purpose

Spiritual Goals:

(1) _____

(2) _____

(3) _____

~ Chapter 5 ~

Determining Your Spiritual Health

"...to prepare God's people for works of service, so that the body of Christ may be build up until we all reach unity in faith and in the knowledge of the Son of God and become mature, attaining to the whole measure of the fullness of God." (Eph. 4:12-13)

A very important part of spiritual goal setting is understanding where we are currently in our spiritual walk with Christ, in other words, **your spiritual health**. It's similar to making the decision to become a "physically healthier you". We begin with determining where we are physically and where we need to improve, i.e. determining your cholesterol level and then setting goals to lower it. Knowing where we are spiritually is vital to understanding where we want (or need) to be. The Spiritual Health Assessment will give you a general idea or picture of your current *spiritual health*. The assessment is broken down into the four Action Points previously discussed These Action Points will be discussed generally in Chapter 6 and then in more detail in Chapters 7 through 10. They are the broad categories that any spiritual goal setting process should encompass include. Just to refresh your memory:

- #1: Drawing Closer to God
- #2: Walking in His Will
- #3: Fishing for People/Discipleship
- #4: Building Community

Take at least 30 minutes to take this Spiritual Health Assessment. Answer each question honestly and prayerfully. I suggest you say the following Purpose Prayer <u>before</u> taking the assessment.

Purpose Prayer

Dear God, give me the spirit of discernment as I evaluate my spiritual health. Allow me to be honest with myself and you. Open my eyes to the things that I cannot see naturally. Guide me as I assess how my life is measuring up to your expectations. Amen.

Before we begin the assessment I have a disclaimer. The purpose of this assessment is to get you to look carefully at your spiritual life. The questions are just tools to get you to consider the issues and areas of spiritual health and evaluate where you are in your process depending on how you answer the questions. Only God can judge you. This is just a tool. There are no actual hard and fast lines that determine your spiritual health. For many of you this may be the first time that you have really tried to assess your spiritual health. Whether it's your first assessment or one of many, it's just one way to help start or re-start you on the path to growth, to Activate Your Purpose.

Take a few moments to complete the survey and add up your points. Refer back to the questions and your answers when you are ready to draft your goals. Pay close attention to the areas where you scored the lowest. These are the areas that most likely would be enhanced by spiritual goal setting.

Activate Your Purpose

Spiritual Health Assessment

Allow yourself 1 point for each "yes" answer you are able to give. Add up the points after each section to get your subtotal for the Action Area and then add the total points at the end.

Draw Close to God – Building a personal relationship with God

1. I have daily prayer time with the Lord.
   Yes   No
2. I talk to God outside of my daily prayer time.
   Yes   No
3. I hear from God when I ask Him something.
   Yes   No
4. I can discern between God's voice and my own voice
   Yes   No
5. I <u>read</u> the Word at least twice a week (on my own).
   Yes   No
6. I <u>study</u> the Word on at least twice a week (on my own).   Yes   No
7. I regularly attend a formal Bible study (at least once per week).   Yes   No

Section Total: _____

Walk in His Will – Understanding His will and developing your gift(s) for use in the body

1. I have taken a formal assessment of my spiritual gifts
   Yes   No
2. I have honestly asked God to reveal to me His will for my life.   Yes   No
3. God has spoken to me and revealed His will for my life.   Yes   No
4. I am currently walking in my spiritual gifts
   Yes   No
5. I pray and ask God for guidance in *all* major life decisions.   Yes   No
6. I am actively involved in enhancing, increasing, growing and fine tuning my gift(s).
   Yes   No
7. I actively use my gifts inside of the church and seek out opportunities to use my gifts on a consistent basis.
   Yes   No

Section Total: _____

Fishing for People/Discipleship – Discipleship and spreading the good news (the Great Commission)

Activate Your Purpose

1. I put God first in all that I do.

    Yes   No

2. I am actively involved in at least one ministry at my church.   Yes   No

3. I share the word of God with family members and friends when the opportunity presents itself.

    Yes   No

4. I share the word of God with strangers that I meet.

    Yes   No

5. I have helped at least one other person learn about the word of God.

    Yes   No

6. I publically profess my belief in Jesus Christ as my personal savior (not just in secret)

    Yes   No

7. I have invited people to church.

    Yes   No

Section Total: _____

Community Building – Community service and brotherly and sisterly love and care

1. I seek out opportunities to commune with my church family.   Yes   No

Activate Your Purpose

2. I intentionally place myself in situations that allow me to help someone in the community. (volunteerism) or in my church,   Yes   No

3. I have a prayer partner.

    Yes   No

4. I pray for the needs of others on a consistent basis.

    Yes   No

5. I find it easy to love others

    Yes   No

6. I do not harbor any feelings of unforgiveness toward any person   Yes   No

7. I actively find ways to empower other people

    Yes   No

Section Total: _____

Total Points: _____/28

Point analysis

0 to 13   Just beginning

14 to 18   You are On Your Way

19 to 23   Growing into a Mature Saint

24 or higher   Mature/Spiritually Healthy Saint

When dealing with assessments there are variations in wording and feelings of the reader at any particular time. You also do not have the opportunity to ask the author for clarification as to what the specific questions mean. Accepting all of that, this is still a very good general guide to determining your spiritual health. By reviewing the total points for each area you can gauge the level of maturity or spiritual health for a particular area in your life. At the least, you can use this as a starting point for setting your spiritual goals.

Score Analysis:

Just Beginning

Just beginning means that you are likely a new Christian, just starting to learn about the Bible and the concepts of Christianity, discipleship and worship. This is okay and it's awesome that you have decided to pick up this book in an effort to actively seek God in every aspect of your life. Starting now, you are beginning to *Activate Your Purpose*. Continue to be proactive and use this book as a tool to increase your faith and the effectiveness of your walk with Christ.

On Your Way!

You have begun your process. You have certainly made great effort to get beyond the surface of your faith. If you examine the areas in which you scored the highest, you may find that these are in your "comfort zone" and in order to move higher on the scale you may need to come out of your comfort zone. Seek out other opportunities to get to know God, study the word and develop relationships that encourage and empower you to push forward and higher.

Growing into a Mature & Spiritually Healthy Christian

You are well on your way to a spiritually healthy Christian life style. The goal setting process for you will help you move to the next level allowing you to get more aligned with God's will for your life and His purpose for you. Be encouraged and be humble, for the desire to have more of Him. However, don't stop! Continue to be prayerful and watchful as challenges and temptations come your way that may cause you to stumble.

Mature/Spiritually Healthy

Congratulations and to God be the Glory! You have a strong spiritual health. However, be mindful that the strong in Christ are subject to the attack of the enemy even more so than the new in Christ. Your goal setting process should include specific ways to guard your mind and your heart from the enemy through an even stronger prayer life, discipleship and ministry. Carefully review the areas that kept you from getting a higher or even perfect score and set your goals around those areas and remember that we never see perfection until we are face to face with our savior.

You will refer back to this assessment in the final chapter of the book. You will use the "low" or "No's" to help draft spiritual goals.

~ Chapter 6 ~
Laying the Foundation

So this is what the Sovereign LORD says: "See, I lay a stone in Zion, a tested stone, a precious cornerstone for a sure foundation; the one who trusts will never be dismayed. (Isa. 28:16)

Narrowing the Scope of Spiritual Goal Setting

When setting goals it is important to create a playing field or "scope". In Spiritual Goal Setting God is your foundation. The scope just means the parameters within which you are working. In this case, our ultimate goal is to develop our personal relationship with Christ though living for Christ and accomplishing God's will for your life. Therefore, we will define the scope of our spiritual goal setting process by establishing four *Action Points* under which our goals should fall. We were exposed briefly to these areas in the Spiritual Health Assessment in Chapter 5. I call these *Action Points* and will refer to them as such throughout the book. These Action Points are defined here and will be further developed in a separate chapter dedicated to each Point. At the end of the book we will revisit the themes once again as we actually set our spiritual goals. I use the word *action* because when we set goals we you do so because you have a purpose for accomplishing the goal. And achieving a purpose requires

Activate Your Purpose

ACTION. Our global purpose was chosen by God. However, we are free will agents. We must be tuned into Him, we must practice, pray, walk, learn, grow etc. We must actively increase the likelihood of successfully living out our God given purpose. The purpose areas or "Action Points" in this book collectively are scripturally supported and I believe that they are essential to achieving and activating your true purpose and living a life pleasing to God. The Action points will set us on a path to purpose by encouraging us to focus on and be deliberate about our spiritual growth in those areas. It is my belief that as we grow spiritually, in each of these areas, we will Activate our Purpose. We cannot help but hear from God when are spiritually mature. A disclaimer: I am not professing to have the magic key to unlocking your purpose. I believe that God can and does reveal His purpose to us even when we are not spiritually mature, ready, or even focusing on His desire for us. However, this certainly not the case for everyone. I do believe however, that if you follow the process laid out in this book, you will Active Your Purpose!

The Foundation of Spiritual Goal Setting:
- *Draw Close to God* – Building a personal and intimate relationship with God
- *Walk in His Will* – Understanding God's will and developing your gifts for use in building God's Kingdom
- *Fishing of People/Discipleship* – Discipleship and spreading the good news – The Great Commission
- *Community Building* – Community service and internal church ministry and accountability

Each of these areas is integral in establishing a foundation for your walk with Christ. I will touch on these areas briefly and then further develop them as you set goals in each area. Remember that these areas represent a broad view of Christian development and life.

- ❖ **Draw Close to God**

    Developing a personal relationship with Christ will allow us to be successful in carrying out all of the goals we set in our lives. This relationship is crucial. Some Christians carry on their lives as "good community stewards" but lack a personal relationship with God. Developing a personal relationship requires prayer, worship and reading the word of God. The acronym CLOSER is used in the text to simplify the concept of drawing close to God.

C	Choose Salvation
L	Live Through Prayer
O	Obey His Will
S	Study the Gospel
E	Examine You Life through God's Eyes
R	Repent.

Setting goals in this area should focus on as many of the above areas as possible in order to achieve a closer relationship with God.

- ❖ **Walk in His Will**

God has a plan for each and every one of us. If we are obedient we will do His will. There are four aspects of walking in God's will, (1) *Seeking* an understanding of what His will is for your life (2) *Accepting* His will for your life (3) *Developing* Your Gifts (4) *Using* your gifts.

Determining your gifts can be accomplished through prayer; asking God to reveal the gifts to you, practicing the natural gifts you use outside of the church by applying them inside of the church, and completing a gift assessment. Through prayer, practice and action, God will reveal your gifts and provide you with an opportunity to develop them for His benefit and Glory. Goal setting will allow you to develop a plan for getting through the various stages of Walking in His will.

- **Fishers of People - Discipleship**

    Being fishers of people is slightly different from discipleship in that we must be able to draw people to us in order to even get the chance to minister to them. Discipleship is a mandate for Christians. Discipleship can come in many forms but basically involves spreading the good news of salvation to as many people as possible. This is also known as the Great Commission. Given that this is a directive from God, you want to be certain that you are being effective in winning souls for Christ. But before discipleship can occur you must pull them in, you must be a fisher of people.

- ❖ **Building Community**

There are numerous references in the Bible that discuss the importance of loving one another as a requirement for proving our love for Christ. We are all part of one body, on community, and we need each other to survive this life on earth. If we truly love Christ, we must love one another; this is what building community is all about. Love is a choice; it is an action. Although we may love our family, friends and those who treat us well, loving those same individuals when times are rough or through tension and disagreement, is a different ball of wax. Loving those who have wronged us is even more difficult. This is why we must be deliberate and ensure that we are not putting ourselves, or our feelings, first when God is asking us to represent Him in that relationship or situation.

There is overlap in these Action Points mostly because they are all interrelated. Each is interconnected to the next and together makes up the <u>perfect plan</u> to effectively set goals in our Christian walk. Although I am sure you would agree that developing a personal relationship with God is the most important area, we need the other three areas in order to develop that relationship fully. Our past experiences, past hurts, background and upbringing in regards to relationships sometimes makes it difficult to accept that God loves us and actually wants to be close to us. You may need time to develop that understanding through the others areas before you are fully accepting of His great love and mercy. These are the foundational areas to Activating Your Purpose!

Creating Action Steps

Before we delve into each Action Point, I want you to think to the "end of the process." Goal Setting is not an easy process. But, it is very doable. The goals we set in life require us to take some proactive steps to achieve them. For example, to lose 20 pounds is an excellent goal if you are overweight. It will no doubt increase your overall health and decrease your chances of getting certain diseases and illnesses. However, just "stating the goal without indicating what <u>specific</u> action you will need to take will likely lead to failure, and an unaccomplished goal. You can probably fill in the blanks mentally if I asked you to come up with some action steps to lose 20 pounds. My answer would be to cut the mochas, cut the Coke and drink more water. I think that alone would get me down 20 pounds in about 4 months (seriously!)

To this extent, spiritual goal setting is no different than natural goal setting; they also require ACTION. As we delve into each area, consider the necessary action steps that would allow you to be effective in reaching the set goal in that area. The goal is the desired outcome and the action is the thing that you will do to eventually achieve that desired goal. For example:

Goal: to develop a closer relationship with people in my church.

Action #1: Get a directory of all of the church members.

Action #2: Set a prayer time to call out each person's name that is on your heart, asking God to lead you to the people that may positively impact your life or that may need you to positively impact their life.

Action #3: Attend upcoming and future events at Church or in the community that will allow you to spend time getting to know other people. (Write down the specific activities that you plan to attend)

Action #4: Invite someone out for coffee that your prayers have led you to.

    I set this example very broad on purpose. I want you to be able to think about all the ways that you could be more specific as well as the action steps you could take to achieve the stated goal. These are just a few examples of actions that you could take to achieve the goal of getting to know more people at your church. The Action Point that this goal falls under could easily be *Building Community*. You have to build relationships, relationships build trust, and trust builds confidence. This allows the receiver to receive the help and enable them to trust that their issues will be safe. This also allows the giver to give unselfishly and according to the needs of the receiver.

Action steps are the most critical component of goal setting. Actions steps are the blue print to accomplishing the goal. The great thing about actions steps is that you can have as many as you need to achieve your goal. Also, you can keep adding action steps as needed to secure success of the goal and in the Action Point. In the example, the four action steps listed could easily be the beginning of reaching your goal – In order to truly activate your purpose; you may need to add more after you have completed those listed above. Remember, goal setting is personal to you, God, and your situation. You cannot use someone else's goals or actions to test, confirm or substantiate your own. Everyone's walk is unique and dictated by God. Spiritual Goal Setting is fluid; it's a never ending process. Just like setting a goal to lose 20 pounds, not only do you need action steps, you need to always check to make sure you are on track. You must also be in constant prayer for direction from God. As you grow, your goals change and you will begin to develop your vision more clearly. Setting goals is just the beginning. I believe that this process will get you on the right track to living your life on purpose. This process encourages you to live a better life spiritually and naturally. Also, it makes us more aware of what we are doing and why we are doing it. If you get nothing more than this, I will have achieved my goal!

    Several years back I was trying to get into the Word on a consistent basis. I wanted to learn more, and understand more about the Word of God. My goal was to learn more about God. In order to achieve that God I had to make a plan. Reading my Bible daily and attending Bible Study weekly were the two action steps that I wrote in my plan. Although a little broad, this worked for me as in introduction. Attending Bible study weekly significantly increased my exposure to the word of God and increased my understanding. Reading on my own also helped a lot, however, it was a little disjointing as I read the Bible study passages and tried to establish my own very random reading schedule. I had to edit the goal and the actions steps years later and even today as I begin my formal Bible education journey.

~ Chapter 7 ~
Action Point#1
Draw Close to God

Key Scripture

"Come near to God and he will come near to you…"
(Jam. 4:8)

We should all desire to be closer to God. We must start by developing a personal and intimate relationship with Him. This relationship does not just happen overnight and it does not happen without our deliberate action. Growing closer to someone starts by having a relationship with that person. That relationship allows you to get to know that person, to get to share your life with that person and eventually, hopefully, to develop a trusting relationship. This is no different than your relationship with God. The great thing about it is that God has made the first move. He has sought us out to have a relationship with Him. With God you don't have to worry about being accepted or whether he really wants to get to know us better because He already knows us better than we know ourselves.

God Desires to be Close to Us

God has shown his desire to be close to us by sending his son Jesus Christ to die for our transgressions. We were separated from God in darkness before Christ died for our sins. Through Him alone we know God personally and have experienced God's love. "Jesus answered, "I am the way and the truth and the life. No one comes to the Father except through me."" (John 14:6). In doing this He opened the door for us to come directly to Him, to commune with Him without having to go to the temple or the Levites and for that matter, to any man. God's desire to be closer to us is so strong that He has allowed us to redeem ourselves, even after we are born again, through repentance from our sins so that we might _stay_ in right fellowship with Him.

Reflection Question #5:

Activate Your Purpose

Describe your <u>current</u> relationship with God. Be honest. Include as much information as you want. Think about the quality of the relationship and why you have described the relationship the way you have. Some examples of how a person might describe their current relationship (1) One sided – I expect God to do great things for me (2) Mature – I expect God to do Great things for me even though I don't deserve it yet I try by being faithful and obedient (3) Uncertain – I don't know really what to expect from God or what He expects from me.

_____

_____

_____

_____

_____

_____

_____

_____

Getting C.L.O.S.E.R.

Activate Your Purpose

If we practice certain principles we will achieve the closeness with God that He desires for our lives. Note that all of the principles require <u>action</u> on your part. They require you to be deliberate about your relationship. Each one promotes <u>purpose</u> in our lives. Remember, this is a process:

C   ***Choose*** Salvation

L   ***Live*** through Prayer

O   ***Obey*** His will

S   ***Study*** the Gospel

E   ***Examine*** your life through God's eyes and not the world's

R   ***Repent***, Repent, Repent

Choose Salvation

> "Yet to all who received him, to those who beloved in his name, he gave the right to become children of God. John 1:12

Salvation is a gift from God. It is God's desire that we all be born again. He wants us to be together for eternity. "And this is the will of him who sent me that I shall lose none of all that he has given me, but raise them up at the last day. For my Father's will is that everyone who looks to the Son and believes in him shall have eternal life, and I will raise him on the last day." (John 6:39-40). We have the free will to accept this gift. We must individually receive Jesus Christ as our personal Lord and Savior. Choosing salvation means <u>rejecting</u> the bondage of sin, rejecting the lies that Satan tells us about who we are and fully accepting and embracing God's grace and mercy. "…In reply Jesus declared, "I tell you the truth; no one can see the kingdom of God unless he is born again.""" (John 3:3)

Reflection Question #6: What does it mean to you to be a Child of God?

_____

_____

_____

Because choosing salvation is so crucial, we must understand what salvation really is. According to Meyer Pearlman's *Knowing the Doctrine's of the Bible,* salvation is a "state of grace". He describes three aspects of salvation:

(1) *Justification* - is the judicial term. Man was guilty and condemned before God. Through Christ's death God acquitted us and declared us righteous, that is justified.

> *"That if you confess with your mouth, "Jesus is Lord," and believe in your heart that God raised him from the dead, you will be saved."*
> Rom. 10:9

(2) *Regeneration* – The inward experience. Our soul, being dead before salvation, needs a new Life which is departed by a Divine act of regeneration. This depicts a changed heart and a changed mind regarding our life.

(3) *Sanctification* – "Being set right in relationship to God's law and born again to a new life". Sanctification is a

<u>process</u> by which we <u>grow in maturity and closeness</u> to God. (Pearlman, 1937, Revised 1981)

I would be remiss if I assumed that every person who has picked up this book has been born again and born again. Therefore, I must take this opportunity to tell you that salvation is free and that you can be born again and begin your journey today. The purpose prayer below is the prayer that you can say in order to be born again. This is an acknowledgment that you believe and accept the salvation offered. Water Baptism is our outward proclamation of that belief and acceptance. Once we are born again we can begin the journey of drawing nearer to God.

Live through Prayer

Praying to God daily allows us to begin a two way relationship with Him. Sometimes we think this is a one sided process whereby we ask God for something and he either grants it or not. In order to have a relationship it must be two sided. We must commune with God through prayer and we must actually listen and obey his word when he speaks to us

What exactly is Prayer?

Prayer is basically defined in most Bible dictionaries as "communication with God". Prayer is many things. Prayer is conversation with God allowing you to express your desires, needs, wants and concerns. Prayer allows you to open up yourself to God. Prayer is a form of worshiping the Lord. Prayer is an opportunity to thank Him for all he has done in your life and recognize Him as the source of all things good.

How do you pray?

We may sometimes think that there is only a certain time for prayer. For example, many people pray before meals, pray at night and pray at church on Sunday. If these are the only times that we are talking to God, we will not have a very close relationship with Him. If these are the only times that you talk to God it will be difficult to <u>hear</u> Him when he speaks to you. Living through prayer means that each moment of your life is consumed with prayer. Prayer is not only the formal kneeling down and the bowing of the head. We can pray sitting at a traffic light and asking God to assure your safe passage to work. We can pray sitting at our new desk in our office at our new job and taking two minutes to thank God for not only the job but everything that he has done for us. Prayer is asking God, in the middle of the storm "what is your will Lord".

Prayer is gathering together with other saints on your knees and praying and expecting a healing for another person. Prayer should be your <u>life</u> and we should live our lives through prayer. Prayer can also be looking toward heaven and saying absolutely nothing; sometimes we don't even know what to say. Let God read your heart

The only formal requirement per se is that your heart be "right". We must pray with earnest because if we don't God will know because he knows our hearts. The words are not as important as a right heart. We always have to pray for God's will to be done no matter what the circumstance.

Suggestions on Prayer

- ✓ Pray in the morning when your mind is often clearer
- ✓ Ask for His will to be done at the end of each prayer
- ✓ Remember to always pray for others as often as you pray for yourself.
- ✓ Remember to give thanks
- ✓ Set a special time for daily prayer

"I write these things to you who believe in the name of the Son of God so that you may know that you have eternal life. This is the confidence we have in approaching God: that if we ask anything according to his will, he hears us. And if we know that he hears us-whatever we ask-we know that we have what we asked him." (1 John 5:13-15)

<u>What does Prayer Accomplish?</u>

Prayer is powerful. Your prayer must be balanced with action. In Exodus 14:15 " Then the Lord said to Moses "why are you crying to me? Tell the Israelites to move on." In the text, God is basically asking them "why are you still praying, asking, whining; get up and do something". Often we pray and we know what we are supposed to do but instead of doing it we keep praying either in hopes that God will change his answer or as an excuse to avoid actually doing something. Prayer requires us to act. God's will, power, grace and mercy, accompanied by our willingness to act, have the power to change our lives, answer our prayers, bring us closer to God, and accomplish the impossible.

Reflection Question #7: Have you prayed for, or are you currently in prayer for, something that God has already told you to take action on? If so, why are you still praying?

_____

_____

_____

_____

Examples of what prayer can accomplish:

- Accomplish miracles: "Isaac prayed to the Lord on behalf of his wife, because she was barren. The Lord answered his prayer, and his wife Rebekah became pregnant" (Gen 25:21) with twins no less! In 1 Sam 1:11- Hannah was also blessed with a child.
- Keep you from temptation (Matt 26:40-41)
- Enlarge Your territory (1 Chr. 4:9-10)
- Make you Victorious in battle (Neh. 4:9, 2 King 19:1-7)
- Cast out demons (Mark 9:29)
- Relieve distress (Ps. 55:17, 77:1-12)

According to Elizabeth George, author of *A Woman After God's Own Heart*, there are additional powers in prayer, "Prayer increases our faith, provides a place to unload our burdens, teaches us that God is always near, trains us not to panic"…prayer changes lives. (George, 2006, pp. 44-47)

Obey His Will

What is Obedience?

Obedience is basically doing what God has mandated us to do, live a life pleasing and acceptable to Him, following his Word and repenting when we fall prey to sin. Obedience is the supreme test of faith in God (1 Sam. 28:18), and Jesus is the perfect example of obedience as He lived a life on earth of complete obedience to the Father even to the point of death (Phil. 3:6-8). Our obedience is proof of our love for God. "Whoever has my commands and obeys them, he is the one who loves me." (John 14:21)

Why should we be Obedient?

Obedience is mandated by God and in order for us to grow closer to Him we must obey his word. When we knowingly disobey God (sin) it creates a barrier between us and God. It causes us to grow apart and makes it difficult to repent. It also keeps us from hearing Him when we pray. Obedience ultimately allows us to live according to His purpose, which should be our life's goal.

How can I be Obedient?

Our obedience starts with our heart. The word tells us to keep our heart with all diligence, for out of it springs the issues of life. (Prov. 4:23). Being obedient and having a heart for God go hand in hand in that if we have a heart for God, we will be obedient. "These people honor me with their lips, but their hearts are far from me." (Matt. 15:8) Our actions show our obedience to God. We must search our hearts. In Col 3:4-6 the Bible explains what happens when our heart is with God as well as what happens when it is not. "When Christ, who is your life, appears, then you also will appear with Him in Glory. Put to death, therefore, whatever belongs to your earthly nature: sexual immorality, impurity, lust, evil desires and greed, which is idolatry. Because of these, the wrath of God is coming." This scripture clarifies that idols can be anything of an earthly nature...it is our sinful nature that creates the idols that separate us from God. If our heart is with God then our focus cannot be toward anything of the world. We cannot afford for our actions to be different from our words. It is so easy to turn our hearts to money, education, friendship, sex, love, church etc (yes church, good things can become sinful if they become a priority over God) and allow these things to separate us from God. As our flesh battles daily with the Spirit, we must continue to pray for God to fill us up, renew our prayer life and change our heart to desire the things of God when we do this, obedience will follow.

It's easier to be obedient when we are in his will. Think about when you were a child. Our disobedience was rooted in a simple conflict of wills. Our parents may have demanded that we be in the house by 10:00pm or in my day when the "street lights came on". The focus was on your safety; it was their will that you be safely at home and away from danger. Our focus may have been to hang out with friends and socialize for as long as possible. If we were focused on our own safety, it would have been very easy to be obedient because our will would have been in line with our parent's will and we would have been happy to be in before10:00pm or when the "street lights came on". This is no different from the process of obeying God's directives for our life. Our first step in obedience is reading and following the word of God, the Bible (which is the next section). The second piece is yielding to what God specifically tells us to do on a personal level. God speaks to us; and depending on where we are in our relationship with Him, we will hear Him. When we hear we must obey his words.

Impact of Obedience on Your Life

Obedience is pure joy. There is nothing like living a life of obedience to God. We may not understand what He has for us and we may not even at times "like" what He has for us. But, we will have joy in the process of our obedience to Him. I have personally found that when I am disobedient to God's words, everything is chaotic and piece is nowhere to be found.

Activate Your Purpose

However, when I am obedient to God, even on the rough days I rise with joy in my heart. Joy is contagious; people can feel your joy and will be uplifted by it. When we are obedient, we are able to fully carry out God's plan for our life. Obedience is an important part of Activating Your Purpose.

Reflection Question #8: How does your obedience or lack thereof affect other people?

_____

_____

_____

_____

Reflection Question #9: Think back to the last time you willingly chose to disobey God. What was your focus in life at that time?

Study the Gospel

God instructed man to write the Bible as a way of documenting the creation of the world, salvation and how we are to live. He prepared it for us to read, study, and live! The word of God is all we need to give us direction and guidance. We must read the Word to fully understand His expectations for our life as Christians. "But as for you, continue in what you have learned and have become convinced of because you know those from who you learned it and how from infancy you have known the Holy Scriptures, which are able to make you wise for salvation through faith in Christ Jesus. *All Scripture is God breathed and is useful for teaching, rebuking, correcting and training in righteousness, so that the man of God may be thoroughly equipped for every good work."* (2 Tim 3:16-17).

- Importance of Study

Studying the word is important for a number of reasons. The three that are relevant to the subject matter of this book are:

(1) It brings us closer to God

(2) Knowing the Word is necessary for our understanding of how we are supposed to live our lives including our responses to issues, how we treat others, how we pray and praise God, how we think, and how we should feel on a daily basis.

(3) In order for us to be disciples we must know the word of God. We must know the Word in order to be able share the good news of salvation. Once we read the Word, we are mandated to share the good news of Jesus Christ with others.

There is no magic way to study God's word. However, your study should always have purpose. Studying the word requires a plan of action. You must have the appropriate tools in order to study. A good study Bible is the first thing you need. It is also helpful to have a Bible dictionary in order for you to look up words and concepts that you read about in the Bible but don't quite understand. Most study Bibles has a dictionary in the back of the Bible. A concordance is also a very useful tool for Bible study. A concordance is basically an alphabetical index of the words in the Bible and their meaning.

Some concordances offer more information such as cross references and cultural, historical and geographical references to help you understand the context.

If you are not sure where to start, here are a few suggestions for how to begin your <u>daily</u> reading of God's word.

- ➤ <u>Sunday Worship</u> – take notes and write down the scripture used by the pastor or speaker. Read the scripture and any supporting scripture provided by the speaker as well as the proceeding verses and chapters.

- ➤ <u>Bible Study</u> – attend a Bible study class at your church and study the topic scripture from the lessons. This will give your reading extra context and guidance. It allows you to not only read but study, ask questions, and dialogue with other Christians through focused and topical studying.

- ➤ <u>Personal Questions</u> – If you have personal questions about an issue and you want to find it in the Bible, ask your leader what books, scriptures, passages you should read to get a better understanding of the issue and how to deal with it. This is a great way to start reading with purpose.

➢ <u>The Entire Bible</u> – You can always start from the beginning, at Genesis, and read to the end of the Bible. Although there is nothing wrong with reading the Bible this way, it's a little more difficult when you don't have a foundation or frame of reference for the scripture that you are reading; Bible study and Sunday messages help to provide that foundation. If you are reading from the beginning, set a goal for how much you will read each day but don't let that be a substitute for formal Bible study or reviewing the sermons from your church services.

- Resources to Help You:
    o Study Bible
    o Concordance
    o Bible Dictionary
    o Formal Bible Study
    o Leader/Pastor/Spiritual Advisor

Examine your Life through God's Eyes, Not the World

"Do not conform to the pattern of this world, but be transformed by the renewing of your mind. Then you will be able to test and approve what God's will is—his good, pleasing and perfect will." (Romans 12:1-2)

When we have asked Jesus into our hearts and have confessed that He is Lord we have a new life." We can no longer conform to the World including its sinfulness and degradation. In that we must renew our mind to think a new way and see ourselves differently. When we see ourselves as God sees us, two very important things transpire. First, we know beyond a shadow of a doubt that we are imperfect, sinful beings in need of salvation and that we can do nothing on our own to save ourselves. Second, because God loves us He will in fact save us because of that love. We have the comfort of knowing that He sees us as his children, worth of love and protection. He no longer sees us in sin but in the light, constantly learning and growing in Him. Many of us still see ourselves according to the world. We hold on to our past sin (and current sin). We see ourselves as unworthy of love so we treat ourselves in a manner that draws negativity into our lives. We in turn allow others to treat us as we see ourselves.

    When we think about Jesus and how he started his ministry we should be reminded that he went directly to the common people to select his disciples. Simon Peter, James, John, Andrew and Phillip were all fishermen and Matthew (Levi) was a tax collector. And even though some occupations of the other disciples are unknown, they were all "regular" men, not scholars of the word of God or religion in general. Jesus came to them, he transformed their minds and gave them the strength to teach and spread the Gospel. If the disciples were asked, before Jesus called them, whether they were worthy to follow, live with, eat with, and learn from Jesus, they probably would have said unequivocally "no, not me."

Viewing ourselves through God's eyes is especially important in the Spiritual Goal Setting process because our goals should allow us to grow in Christ. However, if we don't feel worthy or think that we can't accomplish our goals based on the world's characterization of ourselves, setting goals will have no meaning in our lives; we will not even be able to "begin" the process.

Who Defines You?

You are wonderfully and fearfully made. Seeing yourself differently than the world does is not an easy task. This is especially true if you have done some things in your past that the people around you remember or if you have a criminal record or have been a victim. Sometimes it's a matter of believing God's version of you, accepting that version and walking in it. We have all struggled with things in our lives. Some of those things have caused shame, made us feel like we are less than and powerless, undeserving of love. The world tells us all sorts of things about us and it's usually negative. We have to rise above all of that because God gives us a new mind once we are born again. He gives us a new life. Our life will not change overnight but it will change because it is God's will that we live according to his vision for our lives. You may have to take some time to address how you feel about yourself when you look in the mirror.

It is so important for us to evaluate how we define ourselves now so we can address those issues while we set goals. If you believe you are worthless and cannot achieve success in your natural life, how will you begin to set goals for your spiritual life? I will make it easy for you today. We are all born in sin and are as filthy rags. We all have the same starting point. But God loved us so much that He saved us from our filthy state. He sees us as His beloved creation; he wants to empower us to be great and all we have to do is choose Him. Once He has forgiven our sins, we don't have to take the burden up again. We get a chance to start anew no matter what it looks like to us or to the world.

I have an exercise for you to do. Look in your mirror. Look at each and every part of your face seeing each and every imperfection (we all have them but some of us may need a magnifying mirror). Examine your eyes and the color of your eyes compared to the color of your eyebrows and skin. Examine your nose and its size as well as your lips and how they are placed on your face. Turn to the side and look at your ears and how they are shaped. As you look in the mirror think of all the things that this face has seen over the years and all of the tears that have rolled out of those eyes and down your cheeks. Now, write the following two statements in your journal:

- I am beautiful because God says so.
- I am worthy of love because God loves me.

> "For it is we who are the circumcision, we who serve God by his Spirit, who glory in Christ Jesus, and who put no confidence in the flesh" (Phil. 3:3) When we put our confidence in God we see ourselves differently.

No matter what the world says, we have the power to be who God desires us to be; not because we are powerful but because we are made powerful in Him.

There is another side to the coin. The world can also tell us that we are better than others because of our external beauty according to the world's standards or because of our possessions or our education, among other things. We can become boastful or prideful or even believe somehow that because of these worldly advantages we don't need God. If you believe this lie, then God will see you as ugly and sinful. Seeing yourself as more than you are can lead to pride and the belief that you don't need God in your life. Your confidence cannot be of the things in the world because the world will end and the things of it will end along with it, including our possessions and our flesh.

The results of examining yourself through God's eyes
- ❖ Confidence
- ❖ Faith
- ❖ Hope
- ❖ Humbleness
- ❖ Power
- ❖ Christ Like
- ❖ Victory!

Reflection Question #10: – When you looked in the mirror what do you see? Be honest, look at your surface and describe what you see. Then, look within you, beyond the surface, and describe what you see.

_____
_____
_____
_____
_____

Repent, Repent, Repent

We will sin. We can always pray according to the word of God. "Watch and pray so that you will not fall into temptation. The spirit is willing but the body is weak" (Matt 26:41). However, when we do sin we must have a way to be renewed. The ability to repentant and be restored is one of the major characteristics that separates the saved from the unsaved when it comes to sin. Its part of the mercy of God made possible by the sacrifice of Jesus. Repenting is not only *saying* that you are sorry but *being* truly sorry for your sins coupled with a change of heart and a change in behavior. It is the realization that in order to get right with God you must confess your sin and ask for forgiveness. Repenting requires you to turn away, to stop what it is that you are doing and change your behavior.

"Restore to me the joy of your salvation and grant me a willing spirit, to sustain me." (Psa. 51:12) David said this prayer to the Lord. He had sinned a terrible sin in his relationship with Bathsheba. David had the sense to know when he was in trouble. More importantly, David knew the necessity of repenting his sins and being restored. When we are restored we are able to learn from our sins and move forward in God's will. This does not mean that we will avoid the consequences of our sin; it just means that we will be restored in Christ and be able to continue our walk. The very next verse is also important for our next chapter, it reads: *"Then I will teach transgressors your ways, and sinners will turn back to you."* Our repentant hearts allows us to assist our brothers and sisters in understanding their sin and that God will forgive us if we repent. It lets others know that we all have sinned and come short of the glory of God. But through Christ, we are able to repent and be restored. This is good news to be shared even if it's embarrassing to admit.

In summary, we must know that it is only through Jesus Christ that we can personally know God. Therefore, we must draw nearer to Him. It is with Christ that we begin our relationship with God. As we begin to understand who Christ is and His purpose for us on Earth, we begin to know the true "person" of God, that he loves us unconditionally and seeks out an intimate relationship with each and every one of us. We must trust God's unconditional love for us and we must accept it in our hearts.

Reflection Question #11: Do you repent daily? If not, why?

_____
_____
_____

Reflection Question #12: What things could you do to achieve the relationship with God that you desire? Identify at least three (3) things and be very specific.

Action Prayer

Dear God, thank you for loving me unconditionally. I desire to be in close relationship with you. Please turn my heart toward you. Lord allow me to love you like I desire to love you even if I don't know how. Amen.

~ Chapter 8 ~
Action Point#2
Walk in His Will

Key Scripture

"There are different kinds of gifts, but the same Spirit. There are different kinds of service, but it is the same Lord. There are different kinds of working, but the same God works all of them in all men." (1 Cor. 12:4)

Walking in God's will is an integral part of Activating Your Purpose. According to Stormie, if any or all of these apply to you, your walk is shallow. You don't want your walk to be shallow.

1. Walking in his will means living a life consistent with what God has in store for you. Walking in His will is being obedient to God which we discussed briefly in Chapter 7. Obedience in general is what God expects from us. However, walking in His will goes even deeper than general obedience. Walking in his will presumes that God has a specific plan for us. He does. He has a plan for you, already written and ready for you to execute. In order for you to achieve this plan, God has given you special and specific gifts to use in accomplishing His will for your life.

According to Stormie Omartian in her book *The Power of a Praying Woman*, there are ways to tell whether your walk with God is shallow: If you follow the Lord for only what He can do for you

2. If you only pray to God when things are tough.
3. If you get mad at God or disappointed in Him when He doesn't do what you want.
4. If you think you have to beg God or twist His arm to get Him to answer your prayers. (Omartian, 2002)

Walking in God's will is not always an easy concept to grasp. Some confuse "living a good life", "feeding the poor" and "attending church faithfully" as walking in His will. However, God's will is different for each one of us. <u>His</u> plans are not our plans. How do you know God's will for your life? When God has a plan for us He gives us the tools or gifts to be able to carry out his will. Have you ever wondered what your gifts are? Have you ever wondered whether you actually have any gifts? We sometimes look too hard for the answers that are right in front of us. Think about the things you do well; singing, writing, speaking, teaching, organizing, leading, listening etc. We all have things we do well but we either don't recognize them or we don't see them as gifts. We will discuss how to determine your gifts and the importance of using those gifts in addition to how to set goals for this area of your life.

In order to fully walk in God's will, we must know and utilize our gifts. It is a process and requires the following:
- We must <u>seek</u> his will for our lives by praying and asking His will to be revealed to us.
- We must <u>accept</u> God's will for our lives once He has revealed it to us.
- We must <u>use</u> your gifts according to His will
- We must <u>develop</u> your gifts according to His instruction.

In this section I focus on "gifts" and His "will" interchangeably. The focus is on the fact that God will reveal his will through the gifts that he has placed in your heart.

Seek

Seeking his will for our lives is the first step. We must accept that without God's direction we cannot know his will and therefore cannot please Him. "For my thoughts are not your thoughts, neither are your ways my ways declares the Lord." (Isa. 55:8) We must seek his thoughts to know how to move. Seeking means praying and *asking for God to reveal His will.* Seeking also means actively *assessing your spiritual gifts, skills and talents.* "Ask and it will be given to you; seek and you will find; knock and the door will be opened to you. For everyone who asks receives; the one who seeks finds; and to the one who knocks, the door will be opened" (Matt 7:7). The word says that if we "seek" we shall find. This verse indicates that we must "do" something. Seeking is an action word therefore we must take action to determine what our gifts are.

We discussed the importance of prayer in Chapter 7. We know that through prayer your life can change. When you pray for God to reveal your spiritual gifts He will answer your prayers. Prayer is the very first step because it is our way to communicate with God. When we pray from our hearts God knows that we are open to receiving his will, His gifts. As you seek His will for your life you must pray earnestly. When I initially prayed about the ministry that I started, HER Story Ministries, I was not sure what to expect. I don't believe that I was initially really seeking His will but really telling God what I wanted in the ministry; which is one of the reasons it took so long to get the ministry off the ground. As you seek God's will, be careful not to offer suggestions or ask for certain things; be open to His complete will for your life and not your edited version of it.

There are several ways to "discover" what God has already equipped us with, our latent talents as well as the obvious talents. The Bible talks about spiritual gifts and there are many. "It was he who gave some to be apostles, some to be prophets, some to be evangelists, and some to be pastors and preachers, to prepare God's people for works of service, so that the body of Christ may be built up until we all reach unity in faith and in the knowledge of the Son of God and become mature, attaining to the whole measure of the fullness of Christ." (Eph. 4:11-13) "Now to each one the manifestation of the Spirit is given for the common good. To one there is given through the Spirit the message of <u>wisdom</u>, to another the message of <u>knowledge</u> by means of the same Spirit, to another <u>faith</u> by the same Spirit, to another gifts of <u>healing</u> by that one Spirit, to another <u>miraculous powers</u>, to another <u>prophecy</u>, to another <u>distinguishing between spirits</u>, to another <u>speaking in different tongues</u> and to still another the <u>interpretation of tongues</u>. All these are the work of one and the same Spirit, and he gives them to each one, just as he determines." (1 Cor. 12:7-11)

    I know you are thinking of these as "deep" gifts but I don't want you to get caught up in the deepness of the gifts or how difficult it might be for you because it really isn't about you. God will use you and equip you with the knowledge and the ability to use your gifts. There are two ways to discover your gifts and talents. (1) A gift assessment and (2) Your

Natural Life. Both are subsequent and simultaneous to prayer and reflection and are not a substitute for it.

Gift Assessment

Spiritual gift assessments can help you to identify your God-given gifts for living faithfully, serving God and His people and being an active participant in the building up of the Kingdom of God; walking in His will for your life. Taking a gift assessment helps you to understand the nature of the spiritual gifts, how these gifs are reflected in real life and how they match your current personality and skills set. Having a clear understanding of your spiritual gifts will allow you to be more effective in walking in His will. A gift assessment is just the first step in the process and only serves as an introduction to the gifts. After you have taken an assessment it is important to pray to God for discernment, communicate your results to other Christians to see if they see the same gifts and talk with a spiritual leader or advisor about the gifts.

There are so many areas of gifts and each assessment will have a different set of gifts they use as a basis for the assessment questions. However, the most common areas are:

Teaching	Shepherding	Interpretation
Faith	Knowledge	Leadership

Wisdom	Prophecy	Servanthood
Giving	Healing	Helping
Exhortation	Compassion	Discernment
Miracles	Tongues	Apostleship

You will find that if you take several different assessments, you may get different results. However, you should see a pattern of at least two to three gifts that stand out. The gifts that always seem to surface at the top for me are Leadership, Administration, Teaching, Shepherding, and Knowledge.

There are a number of spiritual gift assessment tools that you can use to determine where your gifts. There are several online gift assessments. We will not do a gift assessment in this text but I encourage you to set this as one of your goals for this Purpose Theme. Here are a few assessments that I found useful:

- Evangelical Lutheran Church, on line spiritual gift assessment.
  http://www2.elca.org/evangelizingchurch/assessments/spiritgifts.html
- Ministry Tools Resource Center -
  http://mintools.com/spiritual-gifts-test.htm

- Lifeway Spiritual Gifts Assessment Tools, http://www.lifeway.com/Article/Women-Leadership-Spiritual-gifts-growth-service

Natural Life

I know that many of you have been complimented on what you do well whether its organization, speaking, writing, sports, financial planning, preaching, teaching, music or another other host of talents. You may even recognize what you call your strengths in life. We usually recognize early on in life what we are "good at". These are what many call our natural talents or gifts. Many of our natural talents can be and are intended to be used for the uplifting of the Kingdom. Personally, I don't really believe in "natural" talent. If everything good is of God then <u>all</u> of our talent is from God and specifically designed to be used according to His will. It is only "natural" in the sense that God has naturally given it to you. Your natural talent, skills or gifts, can be used right now for God's purpose, even without a spiritual gifts assessment. This is a very important concept because I truly believe in taking Action to bring about change. While you are waiting or deciding whether to use a spiritual gift assessment or are in the process of even understanding what that is, you can certainly begin with using what you are good at "for" God. As you begin to use your "natural" Gifts for God, He will direct your path and tell you which specific skills He has given you for the Kingdom and whether He has something different for you. He will continue to allow you to develop that skill or talent in the Church and community right now. Do not be afraid to use your gifts in the Church no matter what they are. If you are a great debater, learn more about the scripture so that you can effectively defend your faith for yourself and on behalf of those who are not able to. If you are a gifted singer, use your talent to praise God and lead others in prayer and worship. If you are a talented writer, use your gifts to write curriculum or newsletters or a blog for the church. If you are an athlete, teach others about the importance of caring for the temple; the importance of health and nutrition.

> *In all your ways acknowledge him, and he will make your paths straight.*
> *(Pro. 3:6)*

Remember that God may have different plans for you than your natural talent may lead you to believe. For example, just because you are an extremely gifted singer does not mean that God will use you in a way that involves singing. He may use your gifts of administration to support the ministry. This is why it is so important to be prayerful and obedient even if you do not understand the direction in which God is taking you. Do not limit yourself to what you believe or what people believe are your gifts, always seek direction from God through prayer; he will direct your path.

Reflection Question #13: What are your natural talents? Identify at least two here.

_____

_____

_____

_____

Reflection Question #14: What are our spiritual gifts? If you already know them; write them down here. If not, take the time to take an online or written assessment and write the results below. Determining your gifts can be one of your goals so if you are not ready for this at this point, you can revisit this at the end of the book.

_____

_____

_____

_____

Accept

Accept is a verb therefore it is an Action Word. It means:

    (1) to consent to receive a thing offered,

(2) Believe or come to recognize something as valid or correct. (Oxford Dictionaries, 2015)

When God speaks to you and reveals his will, you must <u>accept</u> it. Accepting God's will for your life is not just about verbally acknowledgement, it's about "consent to receive it." We are consenting to the gift that God has given us; this is acceptance. Also, we must believe that this gift is valid or correct. This belief is really about trusting that God does know what is best for us and despite how we might feel about it, we must believe it! It is difficult to accept God's will for our life when we don't want to follow it. There have certainly been times in my life where I just had a different plan for my life than what God revealed to me. When I was first ordained in the ministry I was afraid to tell too many people. I was so uncertain about my ability to really minister to the lost; especially when I still was unsure about my ability to do God's will. There was also a part of me that just did not want to do it. I did not want to be held accountable for my actions, not just yet. I thought to myself, what if I still wanted to do things that were unbecoming of an ordained minister, what if I sinned; I did not want that kind of scrutiny. But the Word says *"Don't conform any longer to the pattern of this world, but be transformed by the renewing of your mind. Then you will be able to test and approve what God's will is – his good, pleasing and perfect will."*

(Romans 12:2) Note that the word is good, pleasing and perfect to describe his will. This means that if we accept His will, it will be good, pleasing and perfect. I had to trust that God knew who he was choosing in me and that His good and perfect will would be done. We must not get caught up in trying to understand why God chose you for a specific purpose of why he has you using the "lesser" of what you believe to be your many gifts and talents. Also, even if you feel that God is giving you a task that you are not equipped for, know that God knows you better than you know yourself and he will provide you with what you need to carry out His will. "For if the willingness is there, the gift is acceptable according to what one has, not according to what he does not have." (2 Cor. 8:12) Imagine the peace and joy that would come with doing his will. Imagine God smiling down on you, pleased with what He sees in you.

Develop

Developing our spiritual gift takes time, commitment, focus, prayer and "use". "Teach me to do your will, for you are my God, may your gracious spirit lead me forward on a firm footing" (Psa. 143:10). There are two parts to developing. One requires taking a step back, take time to reflect. Even if God has not revealed to you his specific will for your life, you can still be active and effective in the body of

Christ. You may not yet be ready for what He has planned for you. Sometimes you need the experiences of fellowship, prayer, sisterhood, brotherhood to "practice" and develop your gift before you even know what it is. Allow yourself to be used by God as you try to figure out what your gifts are. The second part is for those who God has revealed his plan to, for those the biggest hang up is fear; fear to walk in the gift that you have been given. For example, if you have been called to lead the youth ministry and if this is something that you have never done before, it's okay to seek help and guidance, attend a class on youth ministry, teach youth, purchase a youth study Bible etc. If you are going to be effective you must work at developing your gift. "For it is by Grace you have been saved, through faith-and this not from yourselves, it is the gift of God-not by works, so that no one can boast. For we are God's workmanship, created in Christ Jesus to do good works, which God prepared in advance for us to do." (Eph 2:8-10) God has prepared us for the work he has for us. It is not by your own will, strength or talent that you will do anything. It is by God's will, grace and mercy that you can even say that you have accomplished something for His benefit.

Here are a few very practical ways to develop your gifts:

- Pray for strength, endurance and clarity of purpose as you use your gifts.
- Attend trainings offered at your church or in the community in areas that you scored "high" in on your gifts assessment.
- Join a ministry at church
- Locate and study scripture regarding your gifts
- Seek counsel from a pastor or leader regarding ways to develop your gifts
- Keep Using your gifts

Use

Allowing your gifts to lie dormant, unused and unseen disappoints God and is disobedient. "Each one should use whatever gift he has reserved to serve others, **faithfully** administering God's grace in its various forms. If anyone speaks, he should do it as one **speaking the very words of God**. If anyone serves, he should **do it with the strength God provides**, so that in all things God may be praised through Jesus Christ…" (1 Pet. 4:10-11) [Emphasis added] There is a person or two out there who has been told by God to walk in a certain path and they have stood still or just refused to move. Rebuking God is turning our back on Him. As we discussed in the beginning, walking in God's will requires obedience first and foremost. If you are obedient then you will use your gifts and talents for the building of the kingdom. Can you imagine if God turned his back on us? Use your gifts, walk in His will. "We have different gifts, according to the grace given to each of us. If your gift is prophesying, then prophesy in accordance with your faith; [7] if it is serving, then serve; if it is teaching, then teach; [8] if it is to encourage, then give encouragement; if it is giving, then give generously; if it is to lead, **do it diligently;** if it is to show mercy, **do it cheerfully"** (Rom. 12:6-8) [emphasis added]

> *May the favor of the Lord our God rest upon us, establish the work of our hands for us. (Psa. 90:17)*

Using your gifts or walking in God's revealed will for your life does not require extra education, knowledge or experience; although that may be the next step. I encourage you to step forward and walk in your gifts and let God order your steps. As you use your gifts, God will provide the tools, situations and the people you need to further develop and be successful in attaining the plan God has created for you. Trust me, if you wait until you are ready or until you think you have achieved a certain level as a Christian, you will be sitting at the back of the church forever. It is important to remember that God chose us before we were even born. Therefore, He knows us in all our weakness. It is not about our own skill, knowledge or ability but about what God has planted and how He plans to use us. We need to move, take action and let him do the rest.

Setting spiritual goals in this area can be a little more intimidating than other areas because it more than likely will require more of you and some willingness to "reveal" yourself to others. What I mean is you may have to actually let others see you "working" in church and utilizing your skills and gifts. They may see you make mistakes, sin, seem uncertain or lacking in faith. This may be uncomfortable yet it is necessary. The discomfort is far outweighed by the joy God will have seeing your obedience. This results in some level of accountability to God and to other Christians who are in relationship with you. The easiest way to proceed with setting goals in this area is to start from the beginning and set a goal for getting through each area; seek, accept, use and develop. Set goals that take into account the "process" of understanding your gifts. Also consider where you are in the process of understanding your gifts. Use the Health Assessment section SHARE to develop your goals.

Reflection Question #15: Has God revealed to you his will for your life? If so, write it down in as much detail as you know it. If not, write down a list of skills, talents and gifts that "other" people say they see in you.

_____
_____
_____
_____
_____
_____
_____

Reflection Question #16: Have you felt an "urge" or a "push" to do something in your life that you just keep ignoring? Think very hard about this and don't think just about inside the four walls of the church you belong to. Think about that issue or project. Write it down here in as much detail as possible.

_____
_____
_____
_____
_____
_____
_____

~ Purpose Prayer ~

God open my eyes and heart to your will for my life. Reveal to me the things that are hindering me and blocking my gifts. Allow people to come into my life that will support, uplift and empower me to do your will. Remove people from my life that seek to kill my gifts. Teach me to do your will and shape my life for your Glory! Amen.

~ Chapter 9 ~

Action Point #3

Fishing for People – Discipleship

Key Verse:

"Come, follow me", Jesus said, "and I will make you fishers of men."
(Matt. 4:19)

Christian discipleship is a concept that was born out of Jesus Christ. Although there are several very good definitions of Christian discipleship; I think the following definition is a good descriptive of what a Christian disciple is:

"Discipleship is the intensely personal activities of two or more persons helping each other experience a growing relationship with God. Discipleship is being before doing, maturity before ministry, character before career."
(Croucher, 2003)

I love these ideas, "being" before "doing", "maturity" before "ministry", and "character" before "career". When I read this I thought it was profound. In the case of Jesus, His disciples were those who followed Him while He was on Earth, as well as those who continue to follow Him and His teachings today. Christian discipleship began the day after Jesus was baptized

(John 1:35-42). According to this passage, the first two men to follow Him heard John the Baptist declare that Jesus was the Lamb of God. Andrew and his friend (most likely John) believed what they heard and followed Jesus. Before long, they were telling others about Christ. Andrew then recruited his brother Simon (whom Jesus called Peter); Jesus found Philip in Galilee; Philip found Nathaniel and soon a life changing movement was born. Not everyone came easily or willingly at first. However, before long, Jesus had twelve disciples. Christian discipleship is summed up in "The Great Commission". After the resurrection and before Jesus ascended into heaven, Jesus appeared one last time to His disciples. This is the moment that Jesus delivered the famous calling for disciples known as The Great Commission:

> Then Jesus came to them and said, "All authority in heaven and on earth has been given to me. Therefore go and make disciples of all nations, baptizing them in the name of the Father and of the Son and of the Holy Spirit, and teaching them to obey everything I have commanded you. And surely I am with you always, to the very end of the age." (Matt. 28:18-20)

Christian discipleship did not end with the twelve disciples and it was not a directive just for the twelve, it is a directive for every Christian. The intention is to spread the Word of God and the Good News of Jesus Christ to the entire world. Christian discipleship is more than being a believer - it's about being a <u>follower</u>! Once you make a decision to live a life for Christ, you must become His disciples and follow Him. You can be a disciple for Christ. Christians are mandated to spread the Good News.

I realize that some of you may be thinking "but I just started this process, I cannot be a disciple." Christian discipleship begins as soon as you are born again, when you make an active choice to get to know God better. Don't feel intimidated. I am not saying you must grab the Bible and start preaching to the masses (unless of course that is what the Holy Spirit is "unctioning" you to do). We can all be disciples. By God's grace, Christian discipleship can be accomplished in several ways:

Put Jesus first in all things

Then he called the crowd to him along with his disciples and said: "If anyone would come after me, he must deny himself and take up his cross and follow me. For whoever wants to save their life will lose it, but whoever loses their life for me and for the gospel will save it. What good is it for a man to gain the whole world, yet forfeit their soul? Or what can a man give in exchange for his soul? If anyone is ashamed of me and my words in this adulterous and sinful generation, the Son of Man will be ashamed of him when he comes in his Father's glory with the holy angels." (Mark 8:34-38).

A disciple of Christ needs to be set apart from the world. When people see us they need to recognize the Christ in us. Our focus should be on Christ and pleasing Him in every area of your life. We must put off self-centeredness and put on Christ-centeredness. Discipleship is not necessarily for our own good but for the good of others and the building of the Kingdom of God. When we understand who is first, the order of our actions is clear. We must put off our ways for *His* ways. Putting Jesus first means basically that we consider our faith in all that we do. We consider what we believe and the consequences of what we say, what we do and all our decisions in life. Putting Jesus first is a choice, it is an action and it must be deliberate.

This can be challenging because even though we are not of the world we are still in the world. We are surrounding by people, circumstances and issues that were part of our "former" lives. We may be in the same exact position we were the day before we accepted Christ into our life. God knows this and understands. The piece of putting Jesus first really starts in our hearts and with our thinking and that must be deliberate. My process of putting Christ first started with a prayer that consisted of asking Him to change my life and order my steps. I prayed every day that he would change my surroundings and help me do better. As a more mature Christian, and as Satan's attacks became more strategic, I had to change my prayer and ask God to renew my heart, turn my heart toward Him and only Him, give me the spirit of discernment and the ability to live a life pleasing and acceptable to Him. Our voice unto God is stronger than we think. We can ask God for the strength to get out of the bed, stop eating certain food as well as to heal our body from Cancer. There is nothing too big or too small for God.

How is putting Jesus first discipleship? People will see the results of your prioritizing; they will see the Christ in you and will understand more about what it means to be a Christian…that is discipleship. This will lead them to want to follow Jesus, as you do; it provides them with the necessary information to make the same critical decision that you made in life.

Reflection Question #17: – Think of your most recent big decision in life. Think carefully about the decision, how you made the decision including the factors that impacted your decision. What role did you allow God to play in that decision?

_____

_____

_____

_____

Study His Word Daily - To the Jews who had believed him, Jesus said, "If you hold to my teaching, you are really my disciples. Then you will know the truth, and the truth will set you free." (John 8:31-32)

We must be obedient and we must be doers of the Word. Studying God's living word compels us to be obedient as God speaks to us through the Word. In order for you to effectively spread the Good News of salvation you must study the word. You cannot tell others about Christ if you don't know the Word for yourself. This does not mean that you cannot spread the Good News if you are not a "Bible scholar". If you have been born again and understand the decision that you have made for yourself, you can certainly spread that Good News to anyone that you meet, helping them to get the salvation that you have. This is the most important piece of knowledge that you can have *and* share. Reading the Word and understanding its content provides a deeper understanding of salvation, Christ and his life on Earth, how to live a Holy life, and God's expectations of you while you walk the Earth. See Chapter 7: Action Point #3 for more information on studying the word.

Reflection Question #18:

What is the most important part of a formal Bible study for you? Why do you attend now? If you do not currently attend a formal Bible study group, what keeps you from attending?

_____

_____

_____

_____

Show Love for other Disciples

"A new command I give you: Love one another. As I have loved you, so you must love one another. By this everyone will know that you are my disciples, if you love one another." (John 13:34-35) We are told that love of other believers is the evidence of our being a member of God's family (1 John 3:10). Love is defined and elaborated on in 1 Cor. 13:1-13. These verses show us that love is not an emotion; it is an action. In summary, I says that *love is patient, love is kind, it does not envy or boast, not proud, does not dishonor, not self seeking, not quick to anger, keeps no record of wrong, does not delight in evil but rejoices in truth, protects, thrusts, hopes, perseveres and never fails.* We must be *doing* something and be actively involved in the process of "loving". This can be very difficult for some of us because not all Christians are at the same level of maturity. You may find yourself not wanting to be in relationship with some Christians because of their behavior, actions, beliefs etc. However, the Word is clear on how we are to treat one another, love. It is easier to think about it this way. Despite my feels, I must show love. Despite the action of the other person, I must show love. If I were to video tape you interacting with other Christians I should be able to identify your love for them in you interactions and words, even if there are personal issues between you and the other person.

We are told to think more highly of others than of ourselves and to look out for their interests (Phil. 2:3-4). The next verse in Philippians (verse 5) really sums up what we are to do when it comes to everything in life: "*our attitude should be the same as that of Christ Jesus.*" What a perfect example He is to us for everything we should do in our Christian walk. You should seek out the companionship of other Christians who are growing with Christ and you must love on them as Christ Jesus has loved on you. The focus here is on being an example to non believers, showing them how Christian relationships and love differ from the relationships of the world. Here we see that we must think more highly of others. Honestly, when I first read this I was thinking how in the world can I think more highly of people that I know are wrong or that I don't believe are worthy of this type of thinking. I also thought about what I have to do in order to be in right standing with this scripture. It's not really that complicated when we take your emotions out of the equation. If Jesus, in all of his authority and deity, could put humanity before His own human emotion, esteem us higher than His earthly life, we can certainly esteem our sisters and brothers as higher than ourselves. The idea is not to put them on a pedestal or give them something they don't deserve, the idea is for us to give up ourselves in the process and focus on our brother or sister's needs first. It really has very little to do with them and everything to do with God.

Part of ministering (sharing the Gospel) is "modeling"; modeling Christ-like behavior. When we seek to model Christ behavior we think, "what would Jesus do?" This is not a just a bracelet quote. Modeling means that as we consider our actions and before we open our mouths we have to literally think about what Jesus would do in this situation, what would He say, how would He react? If we use that model, and not our own belief system, we will be on the right track. If we cannot show love for other Saints what do non believers have to look forward to? Why would they want to be a part of something that so closely resembles the world? I hear people say this often, "the church is full of people that are just like me and my unsaved friends, why would I want to be born again?" As I reflect on the people in my own church, I pondered that question. But then when I think about the people in my own church and consider the Jesus in them I realize that I have to look to that reflection of them, love, forgive, trust and hold them accountable. I also hope that they will treat me, with my flaws, the same. These are the pieces that nonbelievers need to see. To answer their questions I tell them that yes, the church is a hospital and you will see people in all stages of their walk and development as Christians but what you should see is a culture of people still loving and esteeming one another higher than themselves. You should also see people with a repenting spirit, following the will of God as much as they can. You should also see change, progress and growth as you continue to interact with these individuals. However, you will never know if you don't start the journey. I am always explaining that it is not church that we seek it is God that we seek. Be an example, be Christ-like, show love to other Christians.

Evangelism - Making Disciples of others

Then Jesus came to them and said, "All authority in heaven and on earth has been given to me. Therefore go and make disciples of all nations, baptizing them in the name of the Father and of the Son and of the Holy Spirit, and teaching them to obey everything I have commanded you. And surely I am with you always, to the very end of the age." (Matt. 28:18-20). Evangelism does not have to be a formal situation where you have a title or travel to a third world country to minister to people. Evangelism does not require formalities. Evangelism is defined as: "the winning or revival of personal commitments to Christ." (Merriam Webster, 2013) Another definition is "the preaching or promulgation of the gospel." (Dictionary.com, 2014) Although a person can have the specific gift of evangelism, you can see from both of these definitions, anyone can evangelize. The goal of evangelism is to tell people and to change people. In order to be effective in changing lives, you want to encourage people to follow Christ, which is the utmost goal of evangelizing. We are compelled to share our faith and tell nonbelievers about the wonderful changes Jesus Christ has made in our lives; this is evangelism. No matter what our maturity level in the Christian faith, we all have something to offer. Too often, we believe the lie from Satan that we don't really know enough or haven't been a Christian long enough to make a difference. Not true! Some of the most enthusiastic representatives of the Christian life are new believers who have just discovered the awesome love of God. They may not know a lot of Bible verses or the "accepted" way of saying things, but they have experienced the love of the living God, and that is exactly what we are to share. Those of you who have experienced the love of God on numerous occasions must tell others of God's mercy and Grace. Your testimony can save lives. Witness for Christ by your life and words.

> This is to my Father's glory, that you bear much fruit, showing yourselves to be my disciples. (John 15:8)

Evangelism can be difficult for many of us especially if we are uncertain about our salvation. When I began to attend church again, I did not tell many people about Christ. I did not want to be judged. Even after I became ordained I was hesitant to let people now; not because I was ashamed of my faith or God but because I did not want to be held to a higher expectation It's true that your life may become a target. However, you are not called to be perfect, you are not perfect. I feared my own ability to live right and the worst thing, in my mind, was being called a hypocrite. I feared being judged. As I matured, I feared leading people to Christ and them seeing me fall and how that could negatively impact their lives. I could not continue to live in fear; I could only continue to do my best, ask for strength, and try to be transparent so people saw the best in me; the Christ in me. It is also important that people see that you are on a journey as well, that you are not sitting high up somewhere looking down on them as you try to lead them to Christ.

Reflection Question #19: – What hinders you from sharing the good news with others? Does it matter who the "others" are?

_____
_____
_____
_____
_____

Be Fruitful - Ministry

"I am the vine; you are the branches. If you remain in me and I in you, you will bear much fruit; apart from me you can do nothing. If you do not remain in me, you are like a branch that is thrown away and withers; such branches are picked up, thrown into the fire and burned. If you remain in me and my words remain in you, ask whatever you wish, and it will be done for you. This is to my Father's glory, that you bear much fruit, showing yourselves to be my disciples. (John 15:5-8).

Being involved in ministry exposes you to opportunities to tell of the goodness of God and the blessing and mercy he showed by saving us. Being fruitful means taking on some responsibility for the body of Christ so that you may grow and help others grow as well. Actually, your job is not to produce fruit. Our job is to abide in Christ, and if we do, the Holy Spirit will produce the fruit, and this fruit is the result of our obedience. As we become more obedient to the Lord and learn to walk in His ways, our lives will change. The biggest change will take place in our hearts, and the overflow of this will be new conduct (new thoughts, words and actions) representative of that change. The change we seek is done from the inside out, through the power of the Holy Spirit. It isn't something you can conjure up on our own. This change in our life ministers to others. If we are not involved in the ministry, we cannot impact others with our testimony, we cannot minister or disciple others without being involved. I know this can be a difficult step for some. Becoming involved may require you to "let your guard down". People get to know you and your flaws and weaknesses. We have to remember that we are all in this together. We all have flaws and weaknesses. Being involved in ministry may not always be easy or comfortable but I believe it is necessary to strengthen your walk with Christ and to empower each other. The second part of this could actually be another bullet point but I think it's very counter- productive to separate "ministry" from meeting the needs of non-believers. We have to get away from being involved in ministries that only seek to give us something to do, an opportunity for church members to fellowship (not saying fellowship is not important). We need to be mindful of and actively seeking to meet the needs of non believers so we can win them over to Christ. Look for "effective ministries". These ministries will have a clear purpose and mission as well as action plans.

Characteristics of Effective Ministries

- ✓ Trained leaders
- ✓ Vision and Mission Statements
- ✓ Clear goals
- ✓ Clear tasks (action plan)
- ✓ Activities that draw others to Christ
- ✓ Activities that increase faith
- ✓ Empowered participants
- ✓ Training opportunities
- ✓ Prayer/healing
- ✓ Bible focused

Activate Your Purpose

Make sure that whatever ministry you are involved in includes a plan that allows you to meet the needs of non believers in some way. Reflect on what you discovered from your Spiritual Health Assessment as well as your gift assessment as you decide which ministry to be part of or which ministry to lead.

Reflection Question #20 – If you could be involved in any ministry at your church what would it be and why? What specific role would you play and what would you bring personally to the ministry? If you are already involved in ministry, how effective have you been in that ministry? Is there anything else that you could be doing to be more effective in that ministry? Lastly, are you in the right ministry? (This is a question that you may want to answer in your journal)

_____

_____

_____

_____

_____

_____

Let's recap – The way to be a disciple; a fisher of men and women is to:

- Put Jesus First
- Study the Word Daily
- Show love to other disciples
- Evangelize
- Be Fruitful (Ministry)

Since there is necessary overlap with all of the Purpose Theme, as you prepare your goals in this area, focus on <u>how</u> you can show your love for other Christians, share your testimony with others and become more active in ministry. If you focus on specific goals in these areas you will be well on your way to great discipleship!

~ Chapter 10 ~
Action Point#4
Build Community

Key Verse

"Though I am free and belong to no man, I make myself a slave to everyone, to win as many as possible".

(1 Cor. 9:19)

It's all about living a life of service. Serving others is crucial to living Christ-like. You are in fact your sister and your brother's keeper. We should desire to serve one another as Christ served others when he walked the Earth. God made the ultimate sacrifice for us, the death of his son Jesus Christ, in order to save us from ourselves. This is community building. We must be in active in building community and loving on one another. If God can make this sacrifice for us, surely we can practice being our sister's keeper. This category takes careful thought and consideration. We talked in the previous section about discipleship and there is overlap between this Action Point and the last part of Discipleship. The focus here is on being unselfish and loving unconditionally and most importantly, showing that love in your words and actions. Yes, this includes your enemies.

Activate Your Purpose

We are not born again by good deeds. However, as we study the gospel and live a life pleasing to God we will eventually be transformed which will lead to our performing of good deeds. Our service will not save us, but we have definitely been born again to serve. Being someone else's keeper has many negative connotations. For some of us we think of being used, taken advantage of or being taken for granted. You may also feel that others are not deserving of your care. You may also have been burned in the past, especially by other Christians in the body (church hurt). Yet this is not about you nor is it necessarily always about the other person. It is about living Christ like and following God's command to love one another person. It is necessary for you to identify what it looks like to be your sister's keeper; what it looks like to sacrifice for another. There are five basic concepts that will help us get where God wants us to be in the area of community building. These concepts are Love, Service (Help), Give, Forgive, and Empower.

For even the son of man did not come to be served but to serve, and to give His life a ransom for many. (Mark 10:45)

Follow God's Command to _Love_ One Another

One of the teachers of the law came and heard them debating. Noticing that Jesus had given them a good answer, he asked him, "Of all the commandments, which is the most important?" "The most important one" answered Jesus, "is this: 'Hear, O Israel! The Lord our God, the Lord is one. Love the Lord your God with all your heart, and with all your soul, and with all your mind, and with all your strength.' "The second is this, 'Love your neighbor as yourself.' There is no commandment greater than these." (Mark 12:28-31)

Ok, you just heard this in the chapter before. However, it cannot be repeated enough. As you can see, none of the reasons or excuses mentioned above allows you to get away from God's command to love thy neighbor as yourself. We must love first and foremost. If we love our sister and brother as ourselves we are pleasing God. You must "practice" loving others by doing things for others that are pleasing to God, things that are of some use with selfless motives. Love is an action word. Love is also a choice. Love is also difficult because some of us have either been so hurt in the past that we don't think we can love. You may not know how to love because you have not experienced it in your natural life. Although some of the breakthrough regarding

Activate Your Purpose

how to love, will have to come through prayer and time, you can begin with just making the <u>choice</u> to love as God has commanded. For if you don't understand it right away – choose to trust and be trustworthy, choose to serve, to help, to give and to love. The rest will come as you set realistic goals in this area.

Reflection Question #21: Is it difficult for you to love? If so, why? If no, identify the ways that you currently show love for others.

_____
_____
_____

_____

Since love is an action word, how can you show love for another person? Here are a few examples:

- ✓ Volunteer in the community that really needs your skills and talents the most
- ✓ Listen to someone who is hurting without sharing your own hurts
- ✓ When you are experiencing lack – give anyway
- ✓ Pray for others instead of yourself
- ✓ Go out of your way when someone needs you

- ✓ Forgive your enemy
- ✓ Show love even to those who do not love you
- ✓ Say a kind word or give a deserved compliment
- ✓ Respond to negativity with kindness

I know, I make is sound so easy. I am not saying that it will not be challenging. Love is an action. When emotions take over and your thoughts say differently, make sure you actions reflect love. Sometimes you have to move in love and walk in love in order to change your heart. Loving will become easier as you begin to understand the importance of love; it's more about the other person that it is about you.

Serve (Help)

You need to be mindful of those in need at all times. For the very busy Christian, which most of us are, we can easily neglect one another's needs? It's not right but it is easy to do. In addition to helping those that you know are in need you must deliberately place yourself in situations where you can be used, where you can help when needed. This means deciding what type of Church ministry you will be involved in, volunteering in the church and/or community, being part of a team, leading at times and following at other times, just being there and fulfilling a need is important.

There is a notion, especially in the United States, that people are to help themselves, "pull yourself up by your own bootstraps," is often used in reference to ones responsibility for "self". If God had that same mentality, he would not have sent his son to die for our sins. We would still be living under the law, incapable of keeping it, incapable of pulling ourselves up by our own bootstraps so to speak. We would be doomed to darkness and permanent separation from God. We must apply the mercy shown to us as we were completely unworthy of His grace and mercy. Think about that whenever you are tempted to pass judgment on those you are helping or that may be in need of help. Serving looks different for everyone. If you are not sure where to start, start with what you know. If you are a good cook or love cooking, help prepare meals for church events of for people in the community. If you love to organize volunteer to help organize the office at church. If you are talented in writing or administrative skills prepare a class on personal bookkeeping. You may also go completely outside of your comfort zone and join a group of people volunteering in area that you are not familiar with. The important thing is to serve with an open and caring heart; not for recognition or acknowledgment but for those who are being served.

Give

The word directs us to give generously. (2 Cor. 9:6, Gal. 6:7)

Parable of the Sheep and Goats

This parable is so important. It is repeated here in summary version. "When the Son of Man comes in His glory,…, He will sit on His throne in heavenly glory."All the nations will be gathered before Him; and He will separate the people one from another,... he will say to those on His right, 'Come, you who are blessed by My Father, For I was hungry and you gave Me something to eat; I was thirsty, and you gave Me something to drink; I was a stranger, and you invited Me in; I needed clothes and you clothed Me; I was sick, and you looked after Me; I was in prison, and you came to visit Me.' the righteous will answer Him, 'Lord, when did we do these things for you. And the King will reply, 'I tell you the truth, whatever you did for one of these brothers of Mine, you did it to Me.' "Then He will say to those on His left, 'Depart from Me, you who are cursed, into the eternal fire prepared for the devil and his angels. I was hungry and you gave Me nothing to eat; I was thirsty and you gave Me no drink; I was a stranger, you did not invite Me in; I needed clothes you did not clothe Me; I was sick and in prison and you did not look after Me.' "They also will answer, 'Lord, when did we fail to do these things? "He will reply ' I tell you the truth, whatever you did not do for one of these; you did not do for me.' "Then they will go away to eternal punishment, but the righteous to eternal life." (Matthew 25:31-46)

This parable sums it up. We often forget the importance of service in our daily walk with Christ. It is important for us to serve daily, in some capacity. Helping those in need is crucial to our eventual judgment by God. "For it is God's will that by doing good you should silence the ignorant talk of foolish men." (1 Peter 2:15) God looks at all that we do and expects us to be kind, merciful and compassionate, the same kindness, mercy and compassion that Christ showed to us we are to show to others.

Obviously there is also financial giving. I keep a small writing tablet in my purse with the following scripture written on the front: "On the first day of every week, each one of you should set aside a sum of money in keeping with your income, saving it up, so that when I come no collections will have to be made". (1 Cor. 16:2) The text is clear in that it is clear that the responsibility to contribute toward the support of the kingdom belongs to "each" Christian. The obligation to give, consistent with one's prosperity, is obligatory. There is so much controversy over giving today because of the public display of wealth by some pastors of so called "mega churches". However, just because a church has financial or material wealth does not mean that it's wrong or that they

Activate Your Purpose

leadership is misusing funds. The purpose of raising up funds is to continue to do the work of God and to support and help those in deed in the body. Sometimes leaders misuse funds, which does not negate our responsibility to give. If a leader misused funds, he or she will have to answer to God accordingly. God will look at your obedience and your intentions in your individual giving which should be your focus.

Reflection Question #22: If you were standing before God today, how do you <u>want</u> Him to reflect on your life's actions? Would he be able to say that you fed Him or denied Him a meal? Why?

_____

_____

_____

_____

_____

_____

_____

_____

Then Peter came to Jesus and asked, "Lord, how many times shall I forgive my brother when he sins against me? Up to seven times? "Jesus answered, "I tell you, not seven times, but seventy-seven times."(Matt. 18:21-22)

Forgive

""For if you forgive men when they sin against you, your heavenly Father will also forgive you." But if you do not forgive men for their sins, your Father will not forgive your sins." (Matt. 6:14-15)

Forgiveness is not an easy thing. Forgiveness is not forgetting something that has happened to you in the past or forgetting that someone hurt you. Forgetting is very difficult; once something has happened; our brain is powerful and holds onto memories. Forgiveness starts in the heart but also requires some outward "showing". When you truly forgive someone from your heart, you don't seek revenge, you don't harbor ill feelings and you don't ignore or disrespect the person who has wronged you. Forgiveness is more than lip service; it also requires wisdom, meaning that just because you forgive someone does not mean you place yourself in a position to be harmed by them again. It means that you love them, and because you know they may have issues that you cannot control, you may have to cut that person out of your life. However, in some situations that person will be actively in your life and you are forced to have to deal with how to move forward and maintain a positive relationship with them. This kind of forgiveness is very hard and usually involves family members or church family members. When people in your biological family or church family hurt you it cuts deep.

A powerful example of forgiveness is how Joseph was able to forgive his brothers for selling him into slavery. (Gen. 50:15-26). The story of Joseph reminds us of God's sovereignty and that vengeance belongs to God. – "Do not take revenge, my friends, but leave room for God's wrath, for it is written: "it is mine to avenge; I will repay, says the Lord." (Rom. 12:19) Forgiveness is a **choice,** based on our **faith,** that we make through a decision of our **will,** *motivated by* *obedience to God* and his *command to forgive*. The Bible instructs us to forgive as the Lord forgave us:

Bear with each other and forgive whatever grievances you may have against one another. Forgive as the Lord forgave you. (Col. 3:13)

Anger or resentment often keeps us from developing relationships in the body of Christ. We must learn to forgive each other just has God has forgiven us. If we let negative things of the past (or even present) hinder us, we may find ourselves stuck in a situation that does not allow us to grow closer to Christ which will ultimately impact our ability to get close to others. Holding on to past hurts severely hinders us from even seeing the need to help others. Holding on to hurt also impacts your ability to effectively lead if that is what God has for you. In the middle of writing this book, I was challenged to deal with church hurt in a way that almost cost me my spiritual life. I truly felt that I was on the brink of spiritual death when a person in church disrespected me in person and in front of other members of the church. When I tried to seek understanding of that from others that I loved and trusted, the knife was just twisted deeper and deeper. I was emotionally and spiritually devastating. I was told that I lacked maturity and that as a leader; I should have been able to handle the situation. But, I could not; apparently maturity and ability to handle hurtful behavior go hand in hand. I made a conscious decision to decrease my church involvement and activity and was even contemplating leaving the ministry altogether. I did not pray about it at first because I was so angry and hurt; I was blinded by hurt and anger and I went back and forth between the two emotions.

I can tell you two things about this experience. First, the devil will find a window of opportunity, just a slight crack in the opening and when he finds it he will shatter the glass of that window pain and blow the issue wide open if you let Him. The devil actively is seeking to destroy the work of Christ on the Earth. He knows that we are weak and is calculated in his attacks; He is strategic. Being prayerful and watchful, especially in the ministry, is crucial for spiritual survival. I learned that I have to recognize the

> *Do not judge and you will not be judged. Do not condemn, and you will not be condemned. Forgive, and you will be forgiven.*
> *(Luke 6:37)*

attack of the devil and that he will use people, even me, to tear up a ministry…if you let him. I often ask myself "did you think the issue was too big for God to handle?" Although I am more mature now, I still keep that question in my head when I face an issue because I know that answer now….nothing is too big for God.

Second, ministry is about God and his people, not about me. My inability to forgive brought my ministry to a screeching hault! I did not even consider the fact that it was actually God's ministry and my unwillingness to forgive was equivalent to telling God – No to His will. I had no right to do that. It is, was, and is still, His ministry, His will. I was just a vehicle, a vessel that He handpicked to carry out His will. It was not about me. I reflect now back on an early ministry colleague, Crystal. She said something to me during our training "It's not about you." Every time I saw her I thought about that and what it meant. I could not figure out why this was such a profound statement on my life. It was not until this event, which happed four or five years later, did her words of prophesy make sense. God knew that those four words were going to be a matter of life or death for me. Those four words helped me escape a spiritual death twice; the second time was much easier to see coming! I responded differently. I did not seek to interfere with God's power to take care of His Kingdom, and he did. It allowed me to stay in my lane and to follow His will. I was able to rejoice in victory even though I could not see it right away.

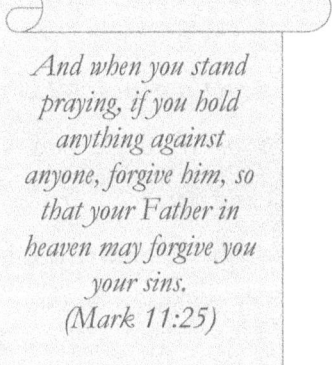

And when you stand praying, if you hold anything against anyone, forgive him, so that your Father in heaven may forgive you your sins.
(Mark 11:25)

Those were the two most important lessons that I learned. My anger opened the door for the devil to get in and once I let him in he tried to kill my spirit, control my response, actions and feelings. This is why it is so important to forgive and move on without losing sight of the fact that God has a purpose for your life. Don't let anything or anyone get in the way of your purpose!

Reflection Question #23: Do you need to forgive someone or be forgiven? Reflect on that situation now and identify it, name it and decide what action you are going to take to forgive or be forgiven. If it has hindered you from doing God's will, how can you move forward in obedience?

_____

_____

_____

_____

You must focus on God's purpose in your life and not on the wrongs that you have suffered. When you understand God's larger purpose, it is easier to genuinely forgive others. God has commanded us to forgive therefore we must do so out of obedience by faith.

Empower-
"I long to see you so that I may impart to you some spiritual gift to make you strong— that is, that you and I may be mutually encouraged by each other's faith." (Rom. 1:11-12) When we help one another we empower one another. It does

not matter if that person is a Christian or not. Sometimes, the smallest gesture can lead someone to Christ. Here I am mostly referring to empowering other Christians. In order to be effective inside the church we must be "one body". There is no "me" or "I" in the body of Christ; there is one head, which is Christ, and we all make up the body. When one is weak and the other is strong we have to lift up each other with prayer, encouragement, ministry and proper rebuke. We are collectively part of each other. You have a duty to uplift, empower and impart wisdom. You may be the one who invites someone to church but you may not be the one to impart the knowledge. You may be the one who ministers to a person and yet they leave the church and someone else helps them grow in ministry. Your job is to empower another. Your job is whatever role God gives you but empowerment is always a part of that role. Even if you invite someone to church and that is all you do, you are empowering them. Even if you bring a sick person one simple meal, you are empowering them. I might say something now that seems contrary to how you have experienced your church members. However, church can be a complicated place when it comes to relationships with other church goers, especially those church goers that are Christians. We have to learn to be encouraging of one another despite where we happen to be in our walk with Christ. How we relate to one another as Christians, as discussed previously, will directly impact the rest of society. Empowerment means giving to other Christians what they need to grow and mature in Christ. This could mean providing transportation to church, helping with children during church, calling to check on people who have not been at church in a while, encouraging others to read the word, pray and use their gifts. Those in leadership also need to be empowered to continue to hear from God and exercise their leadership responsibilities in a manner consistent with God's plan.

"For when one says, "I follow Paul," and another, "I follow Apollos," are you not mere human beings? What, after all, is Apollos? And what is Paul? Only servants, through whom you came to believe—as the Lord has assigned to each his task. I planted the seed, Apollos watered it, but God has been making it grow. So neither the one who plants nor the one who waters is anything, but only God, who makes things grow. The one who plants and the one who waters have one purpose, and they will each be rewarded according to their own labor. For we are co-workers in God's service; you are God's field, God's building." (1 Cor. 3:4-9)

Activate Your Purpose

Empowering is really a sacrificial concept. In order to empower you have to go out of your way sometimes, you have to invest in other people in order to empower. You may have to humble yourself, ignore negative talk and/or behavior or take additional time to help someone who is struggling. It is very difficult to empower if you have never been empowered. However, don't let that stop you because you will find that the Holy Spirit will empower you when you need it the most. We all have a part to play. What is your part?

Reflection Question #24: What have you done in the past 30 days to empower a fellow believer? How did it help the other person? How did it help you? If you have not done anything in the past 30 days to empower a fellow believer, what could you do? Think of a particular person and write two things that you could do to empower that person.

_____

_____

_____

Part of community building is to be good examples for the world because the world is watching us. Christians must exemplify Christ at all times. *"In the same way, let your light shine before men, that they may see your good deeds and praise your Father in heaven"* Matt. 5:16 that the word does not say "you" will be praised for your good deeds but that the *Father* will be praised because men will see what the Father is doing *through* you. God is the only one who *is* good but we can *do* good. In summary, in order to be effective in building community, we must (1) Follow God's command to <u>love</u> one another (2) <u>Help</u> those in need (service) (3) <u>Give,</u> (4) <u>Forgive</u> others, and (5) <u>Empower</u> other Saints.

~ Chapter 11 ~
Putting it all Together – Spiritual Goal Setting in Practice

Its time to *Activate Your Purpose!* Activating your purpose requires deliberate steps…goal setting. Before drafting your goals, let us review some material. First, the reason we set goals is to achieve the overall vision. The Vision is the act or power of anticipating that which will or may come to be. Our Christian vision is to know Christ, to be Christ-like and to be all that Christ would have you to be. To accomplish this vision we must be <u>active.</u> We must activate our purpose in life. Our purpose is synonymous with our vision. However, God has a specific purpose for each and every one of us. In order to activate that purpose we must set spiritual goals. Remember, these goals must be:

- ✓ Christ Centered
- ✓ Reinforced by Prayer
- ✓ Realistic
- ✓ Achievable in a Specific Time Frame

- ✓ Specifically Articulated
- ✓ Evaluated Periodically
- ✓ Prioritized
- ✓ Validated by other Christians
- ✓ Consistent with Other Life Goals
- ✓ Must Include Submission to Christ

Here you will take all of the text, scripture, lessons and answers to the reflection questions and develop spiritual goals to enhance your spiritual life.

Are you prepared to Activate your Purpose? If you have read and answered all of the reflection questions in addition to the text, you are ready! Given the descriptions of each Action Point, all of the information previously provided regarding the writing of spiritual goals combined with the results of your Spiritual Health Assessment, for each Purpose Theme draft two goals and three action steps for each of the goals. The reflection questions in each section should also help you draft your goals and action steps so you should review each question and your response to each question before writing your goal. Remember that the action is the activity that you will do to achieve the goal. The action steps are the most critical component of the goal setting; they are the blueprint to accomplishing the goal. You may want to use your journal to write down your goals or action steps. Depending on your handwriting and the amount of space you need to write, this book may not provide adequate space for writing; especially if you are a drafter. You may have already begun to draft goals in your journal, if so, write those goals in the appropriate area.

Action Point #1 - *Draw Closer to God*

Remember, prayer, worship and reading the word of God are all necessary in developing your personal relationship with God. Each of us is at a different place. Do not focus on what others say, do or think. Think about what *you* desire for your relationship with God and set goals to achieve those desires. Review the relevant Spiritual Health Assessment categories SERVE and SHARE to help you develop the goals in this area. Your goals should also consider the pieces necessary to draw closer to God.

    C – Choose salvation

    L – Live through prayer

O – Obedience

S – Study the Gospel

E – Examine your life

R – Repent, Repent, Repent

What would help you get closer to God? One of my goals in this area was to develop a more consistent prayer life. My action steps were to (1) Find a place and time each day to pray, and (2) keep a small notebook where I would jot down prayer requests from people in church or needs that I heard through testimonies. I knew that having a space and time would make my prayer life consistent and having something to prayer for other than myself and my own situation would also keep me consistent as well a deliberate.

Goal #1:

Action Steps:

#1

#2

#3

Goal #2:

Action Steps:

#1

#2
#3

Action Point #2 - *Walk in His Will*

Walking in his will means living a life consistent with what God has in store for you. God has given you gifts to use in accomplishing his will for your life. "There are diversities of gifts, but the same spirit. There are differences of activities, but it is the same God who works all in all. But the manifestation of the Spirit is given to each one for the good of all." (1 Cor. 12:4-6) Set goals that take into account the "process" of understanding your gifts everywhere you are in that process. Use the relevant selections of the Health

Assessment to develop your goals. Remember, you must seek His will, accept His will, and Use and develop your gifts.

Goal #1:

Action Steps:

#1

#2

#3

Goal #2:

Activate Your Purpose

Action Steps:

#1

#2

#3

Action Point #3 - *Fishing for People – Discipleship*

Discipleship involves:

- Putting Jesus first in all things
- Study His Word daily and spend time alone with Him in prayer.
- Show Love for other disciples
- Evangelism - Making disciples of others
- Be Fruitful (ministry

As we prepare our goals in this area, focus on how you can show your love for other Christians, share your testimony with others and become more active in ministry to accomplish the above. Review these areas on your Spiritual Health Assessment to determine the <u>priority</u> of your goals. Also, review your responses to the reflection questions in this section.

Goal #1:

Action Steps:

#1
#2
#3

Activate Your Purpose

Goal #2:

Action Steps:

#1

#2

#3

Activate Your Purpose

Action Point #4 – *Build Community*

"Though I am free and belong to no man, I make myself a slave to everyone, to win as many as possible". (1 Cor. 9:19)Serving others is crucial to living Christ like. We are in fact are sisters and out brother's keepers. "You see that a person is justified by what he does and no by faith alone… the body without the spirit is dead, so faith without deeds is dead." (James 2:24, 26)

- Follow God's Command to Love One Another
- Serve
- Give
- Forgive
- Empower

As you prepare to set goals in this area think about your current struggles with people, relationships, family and other situations that are hindering you from living your life the way you know God expects. Focus on setting goals that will eventually lead to the resolution of these issues. I personally think that forgiveness is huge. Lack of forgiveness not only hinders healing, it ultimately creates a rift between you and God. If you are harboring ill will and need to forgive someone or yourself for something, you may want to start with a goal related to forgiveness.

Goal #1:

Action Steps:

#1

#2

#3

Goal #2:

Action Steps:

#1

#2

#3

Your spiritual goals are set. You are ready to begin your exciting journey of Activating Your Purpose and living your life for God. It is my prayer that you will continue to seek God, grow, change, be empowered and find His true purpose for your life. There is nothing like walking in the will of God.

Remember that this is a process, just like our maturity in Christ. Even though you have worked hard at setting these goals, don't stop here. Look back at your goals frequently, tweak them, change them, and add more goals as you continue

Activate Your Purpose

to mature. Never feel that you have "arrived" because you will become complacent and that will make it very difficult to hear from God. Know that God has a plan and be open to that plan even if you start off on a different track, He will guide you to where you need to be. Some of the goals you set will just be preparation for something else that God has planned so always be prayerful as you plan and execute the goals that you have set. Keep God first in all that you do and you will live a life of purpose…His purpose. Be Blessed!

Works Cited

Croucher, R. (2003, January 3). *John Mark Ministries.* Retrieved May 2, 2014, from John Mark Ministries: http://jmm.aaa.net.au/articles/8349.htm

Dictionary.com. (2014). Retrieved April 15, 2014, from http://dictionary.reference.com/browse/evangelism+?s=t

Eatons Bible Dictionary. (n.d.). Retrieved from Easton's 1887 Bible Dictionary

George, E. (2006). *A Woman After God's Own Heart.* New York: Fine Communications.

https://www.merriam-webster.com/dictionary/vision. (n.d.).

https://www.merriam-webster.dictionary/vision. (n.d.).

Merriam Webster. (2013). Retrieved April 4, 2013, from http://www.merriam-webster.com/dictionary/evangelism

Omartian, S. (2002). *The Power of a Praying Woman.* Eugene, OR: Harvest House Publishers.

Oxford Dictionaries. (2015). Retrieved July 26, 2015, from http://www.oxforddictionaries.com/us/

Pearlman, M. (1937, Revised 1981). *Knowing the Doctrines of the Bible.* Gospel Publishing House.

Rima, S. D. (2000). *Leading from the Inside Out: The Art of Self-Leadership.* Grand Rapids: Baker Brooks.

The American Heritage Dictionary of the English Language. (2009). Houghton Mifflin Company.

Activate Your Purpose

Rosalind R. Sullivan, JD, MBA

Rosalind is a practicing attorney in Minnesota. Prior to private practice she worked in city and state government mostly on issues of diversity and civil rights. Rosalind grew up in the inner city of North Minneapolis, Minnesota, served in the Unites States Army and the Minnesota National Guard. She graduated from the University of Minnesota, Carlson School of Management, Hamline University School of Law (JD) and the University of St. Thomas Graduate School of Management (MBA).

Rosalind has been called by God to serve His people. She is the Congregational Care Pastor at Proverbs Christian Fellowship church where she organizes and leads small group ministries, works with lay leaders as well as provides internal and external spiritual growth and development opportunities. She has a passion for empowerment through education and leadership. She is a dynamic speaker and trainer with a wealth of experience coaching and training leaders, pastors, women, and small businesses on managing teams, people and strategic planning.

Rosalind is also the founder and CEO of *HER Story, Inc.* which is an organization that seeks to provide a forum for woman to share their personal stories in an effort to heal, empower and restore one another. *Her Story, Inc.* provides an opportunity for women to support one another in various aspects of life including financial, emotional, educational and spiritual. She feels blessed and highly favored to have been called by God to serve.

Rosalind has most recently begun to shift her professional focus to helping small businesses and small churches with strategic planning and ministry development. This is her first book. This book is a valuable tool to help you determine your purpose on this earth. Rosalind believes that setting spiritual goals will lead you to your purpose. Drawing-Walking-Fishing-Building are the cornerstones of setting yourself up to realizing and walk in your purpose. If you want personal coaching on how to Activate Your Purpose you may contact Rosalind via her website at www.rosalindrsullivan.com or via email at herstory@rosalindsullivan.com.

www.ingramcontent.com/pod-product-compliance
Lightning Source LLC
Chambersburg PA
CBHW050636160426
43194CB00010B/1692